WONDER WOMAN'S
GUIDE TO MONEY

The Busy Woman's Guide to
Money Management and Wealth Building

NATASHA JANSSENS

Money. If you don't learn to master money, it will master you. Unfortunately, many women are not only disempowered in their relationship with money, but they're too afraid to learn how to be smarter with it. This is why this book is a must-read for any woman who does not feel confident in her ability to manage money and achieve financial freedom in her own right. It won't only teach you how to be smart with money, it will teach you how to own your worth, take control of your life and reclaim the power you've unconsciously given to money. That in itself makes it well worth your investment of time and, yes, money. Read, apply, reap the rewards - it will pay off in every level of your life.

Margie Warrell, Bestselling Author,
Leadership Speaker and Host of The Live Brave Podcast

Natasha is certainly a wonder woman as I don't know how she does it, combining a successful business, a speaking circuit, being a wonderful mum and now being an author. But I'm glad she does, as anything that helps everyday Australians to get ahead with their finances I definitely applaud. Money issues are the number one cause for stress and keeping people up at night so hopefully, with people like Natasha leading the way, we will begin to change that. This book is a must-read for everyone wanting to get on top of their debt, start saving and get to enjoy a better life for them and their family. Well done Natasha.

Marc Bineham, National President,
Association of Financial Advisers

Having read Natasha Janssens' *Wonder Woman's Guide to Money*, I would strongly recommend it to anyone wanting to understand the world of money and tax in a very down-to-earth style. This book will assist anyone to deepen their understanding of financial decision making from simple cashflow management to wealth creation.

Andrew Conway, Chief Executive Officer FIPA
FFA, Institute of Public Accountants

Printed in Australia by McPhersons Printing

Cover design by Designerbility

Book production and editorial services by Grammar Factory

A catalogue record for this book is available from the National Library of Australia

Disclaimer

The material in this publication is of the nature of general comment only, and does not represent professional advice. It is not intended to provide specific guidance for particular circumstances and it should not be relied on as the basis for any decision to take action or not take action on any matter which it covers. Readers should obtain professional advice where appropriate, before making any such decision. To the maximum extent permitted by law, the author and publisher disclaim all responsibility and liability to any person, arising directly or indirectly from any person taking or not taking action based on the information in this publication.

This book is dedicated to our wonderful Women with Cents community – thank you for bravely sharing your stories, raising each other up, and inspiring one another to reach for the stars.

Contents

PART THREE: PROTECTING YOUR PLANS

Acknowledgements

When I first embarked on the Women with Cents journey, my vision was simple. I wanted every woman in Australia to have access to professional financial advice, regardless of her age, income or circumstances. I wanted women to have a safe place to learn and share, without fear of judgement, ridicule or a hidden agenda.

I didn't fully appreciate, nor anticipate, the enormity of the challenge I had taken on – from the overwhelming red tape that encompasses the world of finance to the difficulty of getting women to take notice of financial matters.

Needless to say, Women with Cents wouldn't be what it is today and this book would never have come to fruition, had it not been for the support of those around me.

First of all, a big thank you to the women featured in this book – thank you for bravely sharing your stories and lessons so that they may inspire and inform others to take a more active role in their finances.

A special thank you to my brand manager Julia Kuris of Designerbility. You took my vision and turned it into a brand that truly reflected our values and captured the essence of what we stand for. Thank you for your hard work, friendship and guidance over the years.

Thank you to all my friends and colleagues who I have come to know over the years and who have so generously given their time to support me on this journey. Emma, thank you for being there for me at every step of the way. Katherine – thank you for being such a wonderful MC and supporter of our events. Alex, Ellen, Yvonne, Alison, Pascale – thank you for helping bring our first events to life and making them such a success. Sarah, you have been such a key member of the advice team, thank you for your hard work and honest, down to earth approach. Katie, thank you for helping me turn dry and complicated financial topics into something easy and enjoyable to read!

To my wonderful mentors: Nancy, Margie, Sue, Patrick and Rob. Thank you for your ongoing support and for giving me the encouragement, guidance and confidence I needed to persist through the difficult days.

Thank you to the industry bodies for supporting my vision, in particular the Association of Financial Advisers, Institute of Public Accountants and the Mortgage and Finance Association of Australia. Although the finance profession is heavily male dominated, I have been overwhelmed with support and enthusiasm for empowering more women to bridge the finance gap, be it personally or professionally.

Last but not least, my beautiful family. Nick and Emma, you are without doubt my greatest pride and joy and continue to challenge and inspire me on a daily basis. To my wonderful husband Simon. Thank you for always believing in me (even when I didn't believe in myself) and for sharing the mental load so that I am better able to pursue my passion.

The Plight of the Modern-Day Wonder Woman

Australian women have come a long way in recent history.

The right to vote, the right to an education, the right to contraception, and freedom of choice over what we wear, whom we marry (or whether we marry at all) and what we do.

Women now make up close to half of the Australian workforce, and there is an increasing number of women becoming the main breadwinner of their family. In addition, more women than men are graduating from university.

And, yet, women still face a number of obstacles from a financial and career perspective.

For starters, it's no secret that women earn less than men. According to the Workplace Gender Equality Agency, Australian women take home, on average, $251.20 less than men each week, with the gender pay gap as wide as thirty per cent in some sectors in recent years.

Despite the increasing number of women in the workforce, the majority of part-time workers in Australia are women. This could be partly due to the fact that ninety-five per cent of primary parental leave (outside of the public sector) is taken by women. Women spend almost three times as much time as men taking care of children every day, and account for sixty-eight per cent of the primary carers for disabled people and the elderly.

In short, the growing pressure on women to 'do it all' has led to the emergence of the modern-day Wonder Woman.

Not only does she now have a career, she is still in charge of running the household and taking care of the kids. And on top of everything else, she is still held to old-fashioned standards about her appearance and her role in society, with women in the workplace facing criticism for trivial factors like a lack of makeup or high heels, or for prioritising their careers over motherhood.

And then there is the 'pink tax', which refers to the extra amount women are charged for certain products and services – things like personal care products, dry cleaning and vehicle maintenance. So now, not only are we earning less than men, our living expenses are also higher.

We earn less but spend more to be 'workplace ready'.
TRACEY SPICER

In other words, while on paper women share the same rights as men, women still have a long way to go to achieve full equality.

It's not surprising, then, that when it comes to money, research has found that women tend to have less financial confidence than men. A recent study commissioned by the Association of Financial Advisers found that women with strong financial literacy rate their financial management skills on par with men who have low financial literacy. As a result, despite being the primary household spenders (women make seventy-five per cent of all retail transactions in Australia, according to Mastercard), women tend to shy away from some of the bigger, and arguably more important, stuff.

Topics like investing, superannuation, mortgages and building wealth tend to fall by the wayside, and there are several reasons for this (which we will explore), including confidence, historical precedents and gender roles.

One of the biggest challenges women face is finding the time to prioritise money management. Why? Because while it is in our nature to be the carers and nurturers, we have also been socially conditioned to put child rearing and household chores above all else. Our instinct is to prioritise doing the laundry over researching our super, in a desperate bid to get through our never-ending to-do list.

Girls today will spend hundreds of thousands more hours than boys doing unpaid work simply because society assumes it's their responsibility.
MELINDA GATES

The consequences of this are wide and far-reaching.

Not only are we slowing down the progress of gender equality through the behaviour we are modelling for our kids, we are doing ourselves a serious disservice.

Take, for example, the fact that the World Economic Forum revised its forecast for bridging the gender pay gap *upwards* from 170 to 217 years! Furthermore, a recent UBS study found that millennial women – more than any other generation – are leaving investing and financial planning decisions to their husbands and partners.

Perhaps you're thinking, 'What's the big deal? So what if hubby and I share the load at home? I do the cooking and laundry, and he takes out the trash and mows the lawn. I look after our grocery bills and he handles the bigger picture stuff. So what?'

The 'so what' is this: Women who fail to take an active role in their finances risk putting themselves in a very vulnerable position when things don't go according to plan.

Divorce, illness, job loss and death can all impact women's wealth. According to an MLC survey, just fifty-seven per cent of women across the country feel in control of their financial situation and have confidence they will be able to retire comfortably.

Of the forty-three per cent who do not feel in control, sixty-one per cent identified low savings as the main factor. Alarmingly, thirty-two per cent of respondents said they have less than a month's worth of savings to live off if they needed to.

Financial helplessness can have serious flow-on effects. Research has found a strong correlation between our finances and our health and wellbeing, particularly for women. The Australian Psychological Society research found personal finances to be the leading cause of stress in Australia. Negative thoughts about money can lead us to feel sad, stressed and anxious. This can cause us to eat badly, exercise less and drink more alcohol, resulting in a lower overall satisfaction with life (not to mention the financial strain this can place on our finances, creating a vicious cycle). Correspondingly, improved financial literacy was found to deliver improved emotional and physical health, greater satisfaction with life, and better relationships.

While it is not unusual for one partner to look after the finances in a relationship, it is not always obvious when 'looking after the money' has crossed the line into financial control or economic abuse – which is actually a common form of domestic violence. Due to the media's portrayal of domestic violence – which focuses on the physical aspect, such as broken bones and black eyes – many women miss the warning signs of this early form of domestic abuse. This silent form of abuse is estimated by the Australian Bureau of Statistics (ABS) to affect 15.7 per cent of Australian women, and can take many forms, including denying a person financial independence by controlling bank accounts, creating debt in the victim's name, threatening to withhold financial support for meeting living expenses, or even coercing a person to relinquish control over their assets and income. It is so subtle that most victims of financial abuse do not realise it has taken place until they are in the midst of a divorce.

> **HOT TIP:** If you or someone you know is the victim of domestic violence or financial abuse, download the Penda app. Penda is a free, simple to use app with national safety, financial and legal information. Alternatively, you can call 1800RESPECT (1800 737 732) or visit www.respect.gov.au for further information on support available.

Then there's divorce. Many women take extended time off work to raise children; when they are faced with divorce in their forties and fifties, this means they struggle to find work. Divorced women also tend to have less superannuation. According to research conducted by AMP, a divorced mother has sixty-eight per cent less super than a married mother of the same age and from a similar socioeconomic background.

And although women are constantly told a man is not a financial plan, Women in Super reports that forty-four per cent of Australian women rely on their partner's income as the main source of funds for retirement, while forty per cent of single retired women live in poverty and experience economic insecurity in retirement. In fact, recent reports show women over the age of fifty-five are leading the way with regard to homelessness.

Therefore, as a modern-day Wonder Woman, regardless of your age or relationship status, it's never been more important to take control of your finances, and create a better future for yourself and your family.

Before I explain how I can help you, allow me to introduce myself.

Becoming a Woman with Cents

My name is Natasha Janssens.

Originally from Serbia, I migrated to Australia by myself in the midst of a civil war, shortly after my eighteenth birthday. Like so many people in underprivileged countries around the world, it had always been my dream to move to a country like Australia someday. So when an opportunity emerged for me to study here, I grabbed it with both hands.

Unfortunately, my parents weren't eligible for a visa at the time, so I knew I would have to find a way to support myself once I arrived. The move was anything but easy, and the odds were stacked against me, but I was determined not to let the once-in-a-lifetime opportunity pass me by.

I wasn't eligible for HECS nor Centrelink support, and the savings my family had were just enough to see me through my first semester of study. The rest was going to be up to me. Fast forward a few years, and despite earning minimum wage, I had managed to pay my way through a diploma in software development at the Canberra Institute of Technology (CIT), and a double degree in commerce and business administration at the University of Canberra.

Eventually, after many years of study and hard work, I achieved my ultimate goal and qualified for permanent residency, and eventually became an Australian citizen.

I always had a thirst for knowledge, and a particular passion for numbers and strategic planning, so I continued with my studies to also obtain a diploma in mortgage broking and an advanced diploma in financial planning.

It had taken me many years of work, study and self-reflection, but I finally found my calling – to empower other women to achieve financial independence, regardless of their circumstances. And so, in 2013, I founded my company, Sova Financial. (*Sova* is the Serbian word for 'owl', and symbolic of wisdom and a bird's-eye view.)

After my son was born in 2014, I started engaging more with mothers' groups on social media, which opened my eyes to the lack of financial resources available to women. Many women were turning to their mothers' groups for financial advice. Often, it was a case of the blind leading the blind, with some advice being plain risky and inappropriate.

So, with their input, I created a Facebook group for mums, dedicated to the subject of financial planning, called Mummy Matters (focusing specifically on money matters for mums), and I began running low-cost financial education workshops in Canberra.

As these workshops grew in popularity, I started receiving requests from all women (not just mums), and from all parts of Australia, for ways they too could access this information. And so, in 2016, Women with Cents was born. Women with Cents is an online community designed to give women the necessary tools to make better financial decisions and achieve financial independence.

With a family of my own (I am a mum of two), I know what it's like to juggle the pressures of work and home life. In fact, this is what inspired me to start Women with Cents. In doing so, my goal is to change the way women think about money.

This is something I am extremely passionate about, having witnessed firsthand the devastating consequences of poor financial decisions. That's why I wrote this book – to help you break free from the herd and create your own financial future.

Break Free from the Herd and Carve Your Own Path

In writing this book, my hope isn't that you blindly follow the steps I have laid out. It is to give you the knowledge, power and confidence to do what you need to do in order to get where you want to go.

All too often, I see people blindly follow advice given to them by a friend, family member or professional – or act on something they read about or saw on TV – without really understanding that advice and considering how appropriate it is for them.

As women, we are especially prone to second-guessing ourselves and our own ability, often to our own detriment.

This book is not about telling you what to do with your money. This book is about giving you the tools you need to take charge of your destiny! That means having enough knowhow to determine if the advice you are getting is right for you, and the confidence to ask the questions you need answered in order to make an informed decision (and get bang for your buck when you hire an expert).

This book consists of three parts:

Part One: Laying the Foundations

In this section, we will discuss the foundations of good money management. In other words, having a clear plan for your cash flow, a simple way to track your spending (and your goals), and a strategy for getting rid of personal debt such as credit card debt and personal loans.

Part Two: Building Your Dream Life

In part two, we'll turn our focus to simple but effective strategies for building wealth, such as managing your mortgage more effectively so you can build equity, as well as growing your wealth for the future.

Part Three: Protecting Your Plans

The cornerstone of every good financial plan is having a backup plan in place, so that you're adequately prepared when life throws you a curveball. In part three, we will discuss how to structure an effective backup plan with insurance. We'll also discuss all of the critical elements of estate planning, including wills and powers of attorney.

Regardless of how much money you earn, the key to financial success is how you manage the money that's coming in. By the end of this book, you'll have the right mindset, knowledge and tools to not only manage but transform your finances.

As the late Professor Randy Pausch said, 'It's not about the cards you're dealt, but how you play the hand.' Are you ready to play your hand?

Part One:

Laying the Foundations

CHAPTER ONE:

Reject Old Paradigms

To change something about your life for the better, you need to change something you are currently doing. In other words, you need to create a paradigm shift. A paradigm is a set of ideas, assumptions and values used to view something in a particular way.

When you operate from a particular paradigm, it means that you have certain beliefs or assumptions about the way things are and the way you need to behave. You may also believe that unless you do these things, you won't get the desired result.

In this chapter, I'll identify a couple of paradigms or belief systems that are common among women, and explain how these can cloud your vision when it comes to money management and wealth building. Then, I'll share some proven tips and strategies to help you reject these paradigms and create new ones.

Paradigm 1: I'm Not Good with Money

In my experience, a very common paradigm or belief among women is that they simply aren't any good with money. And this belief is present regardless of their age, career or social status. Very often I hear statements like: 'I'm no good with numbers,' 'I love to spend,' and so on.

For a long time, I struggled to understand where these limiting beliefs were coming from. It wasn't until I started paying closer attention to the language we use around children – and the different language we use around girls versus boys – that I began to understand the problem.

Let me give you an example. The other day, I was attending a mothers' group catch-up. I went to pay for my coffee with my eight-month-old baby, Emma, on my hip. She was playing with my wallet, prompting the lovely man at the counter to say, 'Oh, you will be good at spending your parents' money! Girls are good at that. I should know – I have two of them.'

Now, obviously he didn't mean anything by it. But these sorts of remarks have been said to Emma (or to me about Emma) many times, by people of both genders and from different generations. But here's the thing: No one ever said this to my son, not even at that age.

When Nicholas was about two years old, he absolutely loved 'helping' me pay for things at the supermarket with payWave. When it was time to pay for the groceries, he would pass my credit card over the EFTPOS machine with a big grin on his face.

No one ever commented that he would grow up to be a big spender. In fact, the comments were focused on how cute he was, how quickly kids grow up (look, he already knows how to use EFTPOS!) and what a good helper he was. Yet, the message I regularly hear with Emma is: 'Girls are great at spending.'

Just as many of us will instinctively offer a girl a doll to play with, or a toy kitchen set, whereas boys will often be handed toy cars and tools, so too it seems we have different messages for them about money.

If we are to be successful in achieving full equality for women – including bridging the gender pay gap and the super gap, converting the cost of childcare from being a women's problem to a parents' problem, and boosting women's confidence with regard to financial literacy – then we must change the messaging we give to young girls (and boys) about money, and the behaviour we role model for them.

If you find yourself thinking you are 'no good with money', that you can't understand tax or investing, or that you struggle with other money matters, I really encourage you to pause for a moment and think about where this belief comes from. The thing about beliefs is that they become self-fulfilling prophecies – what you believe influences what you think, and what you think affects what you do.

Paradigm 2: I Don't Have Time

As women, the second paradigm we tend to operate from – and, as a result, our first priority above all else – is the belief that it's our responsibility to look after the household. In doing so, we tend to place everyone else's needs before our own. The end result is that we carry an increasingly heavy mental load, which becomes even worse once you introduce kids into the equation.

The mental load refers to the seemingly never-ending to-do list we face with regard to work and social schedules, domestic chores and childcare activities. Research has shown that the responsibility of completing this to-do list falls disproportionally to women. A couple of years ago, an illustration by a French cartoonist made headlines because it resonated so strongly with women around the world. Titled 'You should have asked', it depicts the mental load and the household challenges faced by women on a daily basis, even those with a supportive partner.

While I don't disagree with the depiction, I can't help but feel like the comic not only gave women across the world validation for their struggles, it also gave us an excuse. And it is one I hear often: 'I have all this other stuff on my plate, so how can I possibly find the time to learn about money?'

You simply can't afford to think this way.

> *It's not the load that breaks you down,*
> *it's the way you carry it.*
> LENA HORNE

While it is real, the mental load is *not* what is stopping you from getting ahead – be it in life, your career or financially. What is stopping you is *your decision* to let it get in the way.

For the remainder of this chapter, I want to share with you how I, and plenty of other women, have freed up time in our schedules by overcoming the instinct to micromanage everything and everyone around us. Be warned: In order to do this, you may need to change your attitude towards household tasks and parenting duties.

I'll show you how to push past the mental load, how to avoid stereotypical gender roles, and how to make time for the things that truly matter (like managing your money). As the saying goes, what got you here won't get you there, so unless you address the stories and habits that have been getting in your way, you will struggle to create real change in your life.

My 'Aha!' Moment

A few years ago, I found myself feeling overwhelmed by my to-do list, so much so that I didn't know what to do first. My son was eighteen months old, I was trying to get my business off the ground, and it felt like one step forward, two steps back. I would just start making progress on my workload, only for childcare to call and say my son had developed a high temperature and had to go home. Cue me finishing work early to look after him.

Both my husband and I are self-employed, but as his business is more established, I was acutely aware that if he didn't work our cash flow would suffer an immediate impact. So, my instinct was to prioritise his time over my own (yes, I made the classic mistake of not valuing my own contribution). In essence, this decision meant that I was trying to be a present parent, run my business and take care of the household all at the same time.

One day, I finally had a wakeup call.

I was trying to arrange a catch-up with an old friend visiting from interstate, and so I looked at our family calendar on my phone. Much to my surprise, I found my husband had a heap of fun activities already scheduled in – for months in advance! There were football games, the latest *Star Wars* movie premiere, Sunday cycling sessions to train for L'Etape Australia and so on.

At first I was furious. Here I was, working around the clock and looking after our son, with barely enough time to shower uninterrupted. Meanwhile, he had all these events scheduled for himself.

And then it hit me – what he is doing is healthy! It is good for his physical and emotional health, it is good for our marriage, and it sets a good example for our kids. I shouldn't be annoyed with him for doing it. On the contrary, I should be taking a leaf out of his book and doing the same! After all, unless we make time for the stuff that matters, it will never happen!

> *The key is not to prioritise what's on your schedule*
> *but to schedule your priorities.*
> STEPHEN COVEY

For months I had been saying to myself and my family, 'I don't have time for X right now. Work is so busy. But in just a few more weeks, once all this stuff is done, I will have time then.' Months would pass and I would still be saying the same thing! The faster I got through my to-do list, the more work would pile on! What I needed to do was accept the reality that life will never get less busy (at least not for the next ten or twenty years!) and instead find a way to make it work.

I'm not the only woman who, after years of struggling to bear the load, had an 'aha!' moment like this. In the following case study, mother-of-two Amanda explains what led her to take a more active, empowered approach to her finances and parenting responsibilities.

CASE STUDY: AMANDA'S STORY

By the second half of 2017, I was drowning. I'd recently returned to full-time work and was still battling postnatal depression after the birth of my almost two-year-old daughter. Being a single parent of two little girls - and paying for childcare and a mortgage, and all the other necessities of life - was draining my finances. I was only making it worse by overspending and putting my head in the sand about the state of my credit card debt.

I had convinced myself that there was no way to get off the treadmill I was on, because every bit of my time and energy went into my job and my children. There was nothing left over to manage my money or earn more. Everything came to a head in early 2018 when my elder daughter started preschool. I grew up with a mum who stayed at home and was there after school, and suddenly I realised I wanted some of that for my own daughters.

And that became my motivation to change my situation. Finding a way to have a better lifestyle for me and my children, and being the kind of parent that I wanted to be, gave me the push I needed to really examine what was going on in my life and what needed to change. I signed up to Natasha's money boot camp and started taking an active role in managing my money again. By spending an hour less on my phone every day, checking social media and reading things I didn't really care about, I had a handle on where all my money was going.

Then I had an epiphany. I could start a business and scale it slowly over time, with the goal of eventually stepping away from my nine-to-five job. And a funny thing happened. Because I had a plan and knew what I wanted to achieve, I found the time to make it happen. I launched my copywriting and editing business, and in the first three months I earned more than my first-year target. When I started my business, I had a three-year plan to transition to it full-time. If I keep up my money management improvements, I'll be able to do it in half the time.

Lightening the Load

In order to take control of your financial future, you need to lighten your mental load. It all starts with tackling the to-do list at home. According to the Australian Bureau of Statistics, women spend twice as much time as men on household chores and childcare, taking up nearly four hours of each day.

Add to this the extra time we spend each day getting ready for work, by doing our hair and makeup, and it's easy to see why women tend to lack the time to manage their finances. In fact, in her book *The Good Girl Stripped Bare*, former newsreader Tracy Spicer reveals women spend

3,276 hours on personal grooming over a lifetime, while men only devote 1,092 hours – about a third of the time.

Years ago, my husband and I were battling with my refusal to lighten the mental load I was carrying. I was feeling overwhelmed, and so finally I put my hand up and asked him for help.

'I just don't have the mental capacity to take on the business, the kids and everything else. I can't always be the parent who leaves work whenever childcare calls. Something has to give and something has to change,' I said.

So we sat down and planned our schedules together. We agreed to share parenting duties when childcare wasn't an option, and Simon agreed to take charge of the cooking and grocery shopping.

This experience really made me realise one of the key differences between men and women. If you give a man a task, most men will be more than happy to complete it for you. What they lack, though, is the intuition to jump in and say, 'You seem to have a lot on your plate – what can I do to help?' (I believe a contributing factor is our social conditioning, which I will discuss later.) This is something women are particularly good at, as it is in our instincts to look after the needs of others. So while men need to work on being more observant, and identifying when we need help, as women we need to work on overcoming our pride and *asking* for help.

I can hear you saying, 'But I shouldn't *have* to ask – he should see how much I have on and *offer* to help.' I too was stuck in this mindset for many years until I realised it wasn't serving me, so I let it go.

Once my husband and I made the decision to share the mental load, it wasn't all smooth sailing. But the key to reducing my mental load was to allow my husband to do things in his own way and not to micromanage. Part of that involved allowing him to learn from his own mistakes (just as I had).

Let me give you an example. When my son was being toilet trained, Simon and I took him to the mall. On this particular occasion, I didn't remind my husband to pack the baby bag in the car. When we arrived at the mall, I asked, 'Did you pack his spare clothes?' To which Simon replied, 'Nah, he won't need it. We won't be long.'

Sure enough, we weren't in the mall ten minutes when our little boy had an accident. A number two, at that. At this point, I had a choice. I could burst in frustration ('Why do I have to think of everything?!') and start an argument, leaving us all feeling stressed, upset and exhausted. Or I could recognise that Simon had made an honest mistake, take a deep breath and work through it as a team. I chose the latter and together we sprang into action.

We were in Target, so I found a pair of pants on sale, grabbed some wipes, and we went to the toilet and dealt with the situation as a team. Best of all, I didn't even have to say anything – my husband learned from his mistake and the next time he left the house he made sure he was prepared.

The key to reducing the mental load is to delegate some responsibility to other family members and resist the urge to micromanage them.

Why am I telling you this? Because in order to focus your attention elsewhere, it's crucial that you lighten the mental load by delegating tasks and letting others rise to the occasion. This means absolving yourself of all responsibility related to the task, including the thinking and planning, and reducing your expectations. Remember, done is better than perfect.

It took some time, but I no longer have to bear the sole responsibility of remembering to buy toilet paper next time I'm in the supermarket, or that we are about to run out of nappies. Because I was willing to let go of the responsibility, my hubby was able to share the load with me.

However, I will be the first to admit that, as women, we can often be our own worst enemy. Let's face it. Deep down, we take pride in the amount we manage to juggle and the way we do things. And when it comes to letting others help us, our first thought is often: 'But it won't be done right,' or 'By the time I tell you how to do it, I may as well have done it myself.'

Does this sound familiar? That used to be me.

If you're the same, my question to you is: So what? So what if the laundry isn't folded just the way you like it? So what if tonight's dinner isn't a gourmet meal or is the same thing you've had three times this week?

By insisting on doing everything ourselves and holding ourselves to unrealistic standards, not only are we building a rod for our own backs, we are also perpetuating social bias with the example we set for our kids – that mum does the housework and dad brings home the bacon.

Ask yourself: In the grand scheme of things, what is more important? That the house is always spotless? Or that you have time freed up to do more of what you enjoy?

Done is better than perfect.

Make a promise to yourself that, as of this moment, you will work on letting go of some of your mental load. If you are in a relationship, talk to your partner about sharing more of the domestic responsibility. If you have kids, then it's time to get them involved too!

You may be surprised to find that others are even better at doing something than you. I noticed it one day when our baby was asleep and my husband was putting away the laundry. In half the time it would have taken me, he got through a full load of laundry *and* cleaned the kitchen. I believe this is, in part, due to the way our brains work. Women have diffused awareness; diffuse means 'to pour in every direction'. This makes us great multitaskers and lateral thinkers, but it can also slow us down! Men, on the other hand, are much better at focusing their minds on one task at a time. So work with each other's strengths to make life easier and more fun for all concerned.

If your partner already helps you out when you ask, that's a great starting point. However, this still means you are carrying the burden of having to remember what needs doing. It will take some time, but ultimately you want to reach the point where you no longer have to be the one who remembers what needs doing – others can equally share that responsibility.

If you are single, don't be afraid to lean on friends and family for a helping hand, especially if you have kids. There is a reason why they say it takes a village to raise a child – you don't have to do everything yourself.

Best of all, we live in the age of the gig economy, where it is possible to outsource just about everything. You may find yourself feeling guilty or lazy by getting someone else to do something you're capable of doing, or you may think it's an added expense you can't afford. This isn't the case, providing you are productive with how you use that time.

For example, if having less on your to-do list finally means you have time to start that side business and make some extra money, look after yourself better, or learn how to invest your money and grow your super, then I would argue that is time and money well spent in the long run!

Overcoming Unconscious Bias at Home

Regardless of whether you are single and in charge of your own finances or in a relationship, it is really important to be on the lookout for unconscious social bias that can cause you to self-sabotage your progress and independence. It can sneak up on you without you even realising.

Unconscious biases are social stereotypes about certain groups of people that individuals form outside their own conscious awareness. Everyone holds unconscious beliefs about various social and identity groups, and these biases stem from our tendency to organise social worlds by categorising.

Unconscious bias is far more prevalent than conscious prejudice and often incompatible with our conscious values. Certain scenarios can activate unconscious attitudes and beliefs. For example, biases may be more prevalent when multitasking or working under pressure.

I believe unconscious social bias is one of the reasons most men don't volunteer to help with the housework. Chances are, this is how they grew up. Mum doing everything around the house is seen as the norm. Even as kids, it probably never occurred to us to ask if she needed a helping hand. It is not something we intentionally ignore. Just like gravity, it is so normal that it simply goes unnoticed.

Let me give you another example of how unconscious bias can affect our behaviour in a relationship. I used to be an IT geek. In fact, the first qualification I obtained after high school was a diploma in software development. This was back in the late nineties, when ninety-nine per cent of IT graduates were men (needless to say, finding a date on a Friday night wasn't an issue).

I used to know how to dismantle a computer, put it back together, write code, connect cables – you name it! Yet, these days, I often catch myself turning to my husband and asking, 'How do I work this app?' or 'Can you fix the Wi-Fi?'

How did this happen? How did I go from being an independent woman and tech geek to someone who can't work the universal remote without her husband's help?

Well, once we moved in together, without any conscious effort on either of our parts, we slid into stereotypical gender roles (one being that men look after all the gadgets in the house!). And, over time, I gradually started to defer every IT-related decision, action and task to my husband, without even giving it a go first.

This is called learned helplessness, whereby a person believes that he or she is helpless in a certain situation and, therefore, gives up without even trying. Men typically suffer from it when it comes to things like household chores, whereas women often tend to suffer from it in the context of money management. This means that women who were once financially savvy risk stepping back from making major financial decisions, simply because they've found a partner.

So, if you find yourself slipping into stereotypical gender roles (such as you doing the cooking and your partner fixing things around the house), make a conscious effort to take turns completing household tasks and swap some responsibilities. Not only will it be good for your relationship, but it will also help to shift society's norms and set a different example for future generations.

It's Time to Make a Change

Like most things in life, working on your finances takes time and focus, and, unfortunately, not enough people make the time, regardless of their gender. Living in such a fast-paced society, we tend to lead busy lives with jam-packed schedules. As a result, we start reacting to what life throws at us, rather than being in control.

Without us even realising, we prioritise the things that *do not* improve our financial future over things that *do*.

> *You'll never change your life until you change something you do daily.*
> *The secret to your success is found in your daily routine.*
> JOHN C MAXWELL

For example, we prioritise housework over budgeting. And while we carve out time at the end of each day to watch TV, peruse social media or read a book, rarely do we set aside time for managing our finances. We are happy to spend hours browsing the shops looking for that perfect outfit, yet we lack the same level of patience when it comes to selling off our stuff on Gumtree.

To change something about your life for the better, you need to change something you are currently doing. Among other things, this means carving out time to look after and improve your finances.

Think of your household like a business. Countless businesses have failed over the years because the owners were too busy working *in* the business instead of working *on* it. For a business to succeed, it needs to be managed with strategy and direction, and the same goes for your finances.

If you want your household and finances to succeed,
you need to work on them rather than in them.

ACTION ITEM: CARVE OUT TIME FOR FINANCE IN THREE SIMPLE STEPS

The idea here is to set aside at least thirty minutes for yourself every day, without adding to your already busy schedule. You can use this time to clear your head, get organised, work on your finances and track your financial goals. Here's how you do it:

STEP 1: Write up your to-do list for the week and apply this information to a weekly calendar. Be as detailed as you can. Include any events you have to attend, chores that you need to complete, and anything else you're likely to do – even if it seems trivial (like watching your favourite TV shows or scrolling through Facebook).

STEP 2: Cull! Look at what tasks you can skip, postpone or delegate. Once you've done this, your schedule should be less busy.

STEP 3: Looking at the gaps in your schedule, allocate at least thirty minutes of each day to your finances. Make it a non-negotiable task to complete every day.

In later chapters, I'll explain exactly how you can use this time to better manage your finances.

Chapter Summary

Women face plenty of obstacles when it comes to money. The biggest challenge we face is overcoming the mental load and learning to make time for our finances.

The key to tackling the mental load is becoming resourceful and allowing others – particularly our partners – to help us with some of the mundane daily tasks we all have to complete.

No one else will do this for you. If you want to get ahead financially, you have to make it your focus and carve out time in your schedule to devote to your finances.

CHAPTER TWO:

Strategise Your Money

Now that you have carved out some time to manage your finances, the next step is to gain a better understanding of your money mindset and behaviour, so that you can position yourself to successfully achieve your financial goals.

You may not realise it, but your psychology has a huge impact on how you handle money. In fact, decades of research in behavioural economics have found that, left to our own devices, human beings make terrible money managers (it's true!). This is because our primal instincts and psychology naturally lead us to do the *opposite* of what we need to do in order to create wealth.

> *Personal finance is only twenty per cent knowledge*
> *and eighty per cent behaviour.*
> DAVE RAMSAY

There are some key reasons for this:

- **We follow the pack**

  Investment markets perfectly demonstrate our herd mentality. In an ideal world, the key to successful investing is to buy low and sell high, right? However, human beings are social creatures, which means we have a tendency to follow the pack and do what everyone else is doing.

As a result, we sell when everyone else is selling (meaning prices are plummeting), or buy when everyone else is buying (meaning prices are skyrocketing).

- **We are paralysed by fear**

 Fear is another significant mental component. While fear is a natural instinct, designed to protect you from harm and keep you safe, in the modern era it is often misplaced and can act as a hindrance.

 For example, I often hear clients talk about how they inherited a lump sum but, out of fear of making the wrong decision, they haven't done anything with the money – it has just been sitting in a savings account. Many people are often afraid to change jobs, negotiate a pay rise or apply for a promotion. Perhaps moving somewhere more affordable would be good for you financially, but fear of change keeps you stuck where you are.

 As Margie Warrell put it in her book *Brave*, 'Fear is a powerful emotion wired into our psychological DNA to protect us from pain... it's only by discerning the legitimate fears that are serving us from the imagined and sensationalised ones that aren't that we can forge the deeply authentic, meaningful and truthful lives we yearn to live.'

- **We are more emotional than logical**

 Many of our financial decisions are driven more by emotions than logic. For example, when shopping online, have you ever spent more than you planned just to save on shipping costs? If you have, you are not alone. The Australian Retailers Association has found that sixty-six per cent of online shoppers will spend more than they planned to, just to save on shipping.

 What about buying something because the bargain was too good to pass up – even though it's not something you really need? And let's not forget about retail therapy – we spend when we are happy (to celebrate) and we spend when we are sad or stressed (whether that's on clothing, food, alcohol or holidays) in a bid to make ourselves feel better.

- **We accept the status quo**

  One of the biggest culprits when it comes to managing our finances is status quo bias, which is a preference for the current state of affairs (some refer to it as the lazy tax). This is something retailers and service providers are keenly aware of, which is why they'll typically offer you their most profitable product upfront and save their best discounts for new customers only. Just stop and think – how many things have you left on autopilot? How many times have you taken whatever product has been offered to you? We don't often change service providers, even though we stand to get a better deal elsewhere.

  In my experience, most customers taking out a mortgage go for the thirty-year mortgage, even when refinancing, simply because this is the default option. The same goes for superannuation. The majority of people keep their super in their employer's choice of fund and never take the time to investigate if this is the best option for them. Ultimately, a lot of this behaviour comes down to an underlying dislike of making decisions and fear of making the wrong one (although we tell ourselves a range of stories to justify our inaction, like: 'I don't have the time,' or 'It probably won't save me much money anyway.').

As you can see, to get ahead financially, it is really important to identify the role your psychology has played in your financial decision making. Where has it benefited you? Where has it held you back?

The key lesson here is that if you want to be better with money, it is going to take a conscious effort to get there. Your financial situation won't miraculously improve on its own. In this chapter, I'll explain why it's so important to put in place a financial plan, before revealing seven key components your financial plan should contain and why. I'll also show you how to pinpoint your financial goals and values, and share some tips for budgeting and debt management (two of the key components of your financial plan) to keep you on track.

Planning to Succeed

You've probably heard the saying: 'Failing to plan is planning to fail.' And, yet, so many people fail to take the time to think strategically about their finances. According to research by the Financial Planning Association of Australia, almost three quarters of Australians find planning their life hard, with Generation X and Generation Y most likely to struggle. Yet, this is a key step towards achieving financial success, with research showing that Australians who reported themselves as 'living the dream' are almost five times more likely than the average Australian to plan and stick to the plans they have made.

In my experience, most people approach their finances in a similar way to driving a car. They are so focused on what is immediately in front of them that they fail to take in the bigger picture. This is how five-car pileups happen. Because each driver is on autopilot, only focused on the car in front of them, no one has noticed what is up ahead and taken corrective action. If drivers took in more of their surroundings, they might notice the congestion up ahead, or roadworks, and take corrective measures, such as slowing down earlier than usual or taking a different route.

Getting ahead financially means being strategic about what you do with the money that's coming in.

The same rule applies to your finances. If you fail to take a big-picture view of your money, you're much more likely to run into trouble. That's why you need an overarching financial plan.

Don't allow your level of income or personal circumstances to convince you that you can't get ahead. This simply isn't true. Yet, it's an excuse I hear often: 'I don't have any money to manage.' You may not have any *investments* to manage, but if you have any form of income, then you most certainly have money to manage. Getting ahead financially means being strategic about what you do with the money that's coming in.

Ideally, your financial plan should encapsulate six core areas: budgeting, protection, investment, debt management, superannuation and estate planning.

Your financial plan

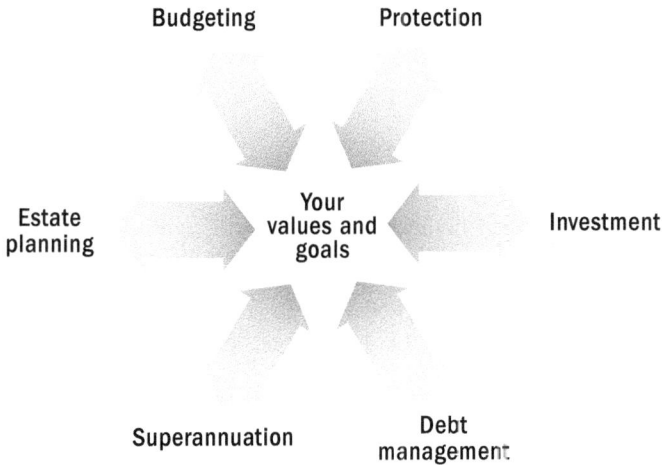

By addressing each of these areas, you will ensure that you are putting your hard-earned money to good use, have a backup plan for those times when life throws you a curveball, and are growing your wealth for the future. There is no particular order you need to tackle these in. However, pinpointing your goals and values beforehand will help you determine which areas need the most attention.

Pinpointing Your Values and Goals

You will notice that, at the heart of the financial plan, there is a seventh area. Your financial plan should be underpinned by your goals and values. What do you want out of life? What is truly important to you? Most people fail to give appropriate consideration to this. As a result, not only do they wind up with a scattergun approach to their finances, they also risk achieving the exact opposite of what is really important to them.

A typical example of this is when I talk to couples with young kids or who are planning to start a family. They tell me that, ultimately, what is really important to them is being able to spend time with family, the freedom to work less and so on. Yet, when we take a look at their finances and the decisions they have been making, they have actually been achieving the exact opposite!

For example, as soon as a baby is on the way, most people (understandably) want to upgrade their home and car – even though a baby doesn't need a fancy, new, four-bedroom house or the latest SUV. So, right at the time when their income will be reducing and their expenses increasing, many people decide to get into more debt (with a new car, a bigger house and so on).

The goal isn't more money. The goal is
living life on your terms.
CHRIS BROGAN

The end result is that this stretches them out financially – forcing them to work long hours (potentially in a job they hate, but one that pays well so they stick with it). This creates a V-shaped formation – with your values and goals to one side, and your reality to the other.

That's why I encourage you to stop and reflect on your goals and values, and prioritise what really matters. Leather car seats or less time at work? Understanding your goals and values will make it much easier to make financial decisions.

> ### ACTION ITEM: SET GOALS AND IDENTIFY YOUR MOTIVES
>
> The following exercises will help to uncover your core values, beliefs and priorities. Keep your answers in a safe place to refer back to as you need. Each time you are faced with a decision – whether it is to set a goal or decide whether or not to take action – check in with your answers. Ask yourself: 'How does this align with what really matters to me? Will it bring me closer to my goal or drive me further away?'
>
> **STEP 1:** Describe your ideal lifestyle
>
> Grab a cuppa or go for a walk. Find a few minutes of quiet time to yourself and imagine your ideal lifestyle. What does that look like? What would you be doing more of and what would you be doing less of? Write it down.
>
> **STEP 2:** Write down your top three values. What is most important to you in life?
>
> This can be a hard question to answer, so here are a few value statements to get you started. Feel free to add your own as well.

Rank them in order from most important to least important and then write down your top three.

____ It is important to me to have time to spend with my family and friends

____ It is important to me to have time to myself

____ It is important to me to have nice things

____ It is important to me to be debt free

____ It is important to me to have a career I enjoy

____ It is important to me to give back to my community

____ It is important to me to have freedom to choose how much I work

____ It is important to me to be well educated

____ It is important to me to own my home

____ It is important to me to own my car

____ It is important to me to preserve my health

____ It is important to me to travel

1. _____

2. _____

3. _____

STEP 3: Set some lifestyle goals

Using your responses from step two as a guide, it is time to set some lifestyle goals. What are some short-term (up to twelve months), medium-term (two to six years) and long-term (seven-plus years) lifestyle goals you are committed to right now?

Why are these goals important to you? How will you feel once you've achieved them?

STEP 4: Attach a financial goal to each lifestyle goal

Hint: Make these goals SMART (specific, measurable, achievable, relevant and time bound).

For example: My short-term goal is to stop worrying about paying the bills. In order to make this possible, I need to save up $1,000 in twelve months. My long-term goal is to be mortgage free in ten years. In order to do this, I need to pay an extra $150,000 over the next ten years.

STEP 5: Break it down

Now that you have specific amounts and timeframes in mind, break each goal down further into weekly, fortnightly or monthly amounts (depending on how often you get paid). This way, you have a clear target to aim for with each pay cheque.

For example: If you wish to save up $1,000 in twelve months, that means making room in your cash flow so you can set aside nineteen dollars each week. If you wish to pay $150,000 off your mortgage in ten years, that means paying an extra $288 each week into your home loan.

Managing Your Cash Flow

Now that you have an idea of your short-, medium- and long-term goals, the next step is conducting a review of your cash flow to understand what you are spending your money on, and then creating a budget (or spending plan) that factors in these lifestyle goals. While this sounds simple enough, and most people understand the concept of creating a budget, research shows the vast majority of people don't stick to it, usually due to impulse (or unplanned) spending.

> *Beware of little expenses.*
> *A small leak will sink a great ship.*
> BENJAMIN FRANKLIN

Let me show you how quickly these little purchases can add up if you don't keep a close eye on them.

Yesterday, I caught up with a friend for coffee. Four dollars.

Oh, and I had cake. Six dollars.

Then I took my son to the mall and saw a cute little T-shirt on special. Fifteen dollars.

On the way home from work, it was my husband's turn. He filled up the car with petrol – and bought a packet of chips and a drink. Eight dollars.

By the time dinnertime rolled around, both hubby and I felt too tired to cook, so we ordered takeaway. Forty dollars.

So, one day – and over seventy dollars in incidentals.

Now, you may be thinking, 'Well, a girl's gotta see her friends and a man's gotta eat.' I get that – and I'm all for giving yourself a little treat.

The problem is, if you're not careful, it is very easy to do this on a regular or even daily basis, and this is where it can become a problem.

So, how do you rein in your spending? Firstly, you have to identify the cause, or causes, of your overspending. Having spent years observing my own spending habits, as well as those of the women I've worked with, I've discovered that overspending usually boils down to one of three things.

1. Disorganisation

Perhaps you haven't had time to meal plan, so you grab a quick takeaway on the way home, or maybe you're always running late or your paperwork isn't well organised and you forget to pay the bills on time. Whatever the reason, a lack of organisation can be a big drain on your bank account.

2. Habits

These are things you do on autopilot, without even giving them a second thought. Things like picking up snacks at the service station, catching up with friends for brunch every Saturday or grabbing that morning coffee with your workmates every day – they're all things you've 'just always done'. But they can seriously hurt your saving efforts, particularly because you do them without question.

3. Emotions

Your emotions have a lot to answer for when it comes to spending money. We feel bored, we spend. We feel happy, we spend. We feel sad, we spend. From personal experience, I know all too well the impact our emotional state can have on our finances.

A few years ago, I was working in a corporate role that paid well but one that I didn't enjoy. While I waited for things to improve, I indulged in some pretty serious retail therapy, which I justified as necessary. My husband and I planned overseas holidays (we work hard, so we deserve a break, right?), I bought designer clothes (I need to look professional), a nice new car (I need a way to get to and from work) – you name it. I bought all this to reward myself for my years of hard work in a job I hated.

Then I got sick – so sick that I had to stop working for extended periods of time, and I had to quit my corporate role. I started going to yoga, studied Swedish massage, spent more time with my friends, and eventually took up a part-time position as a receptionist so I could take things easy.

What I also took was a giant pay cut. But, strangely, after a few months, I actually seemed to have more money in my bank account. Why? Well, I was happier. I was calm and content, and I was enjoying my life and my work. As a result, I didn't feel the need to spend money on expensive clothes, cars and holidays to make me feel fulfilled.

> *It's not your salary that makes you rich,*
> *it's your spending habits.*
> CHARLES JAFFE

ACTION ITEM: A SIMPLE TASK TO BETTER UNDERSTAND YOUR SPENDING HABITS

To master your spending, you need to understand your 'why'. Why are you spending your money the way you are now? Is it necessary or is it a habit? Is it purposeful or is it impulsive?

STEP 1: Identify what you are spending your money on

Pull out your receipts and bank statements from the past week and make a note of what you spent your money on and why (for the

---

purpose of this exercise, you can disregard your necessary costs, such as mortgage, rent and groceries, and instead focus on your daily lifestyle expenses such as shopping, going out for meals, getting takeaway and so on).

HOT TIP: Try to avoid simply making a mental note of what you spent. It never works! The true power in identifying how much you spend, and why, comes from writing things down and having the cold, hard facts staring right back at you.

Here's an example of how your spending log might look on a particular day. Try and categorise each item based on whether it's a habit, the result of being disorganised or emotionally driven.

Item	Habit	Disorganisation	Emotional
Coffee	$5		
Takeaway		$30	
Cute top			$40
Sheets on sale			$50
Total	$5	$30	$90

STEP 2: Identify the biggest trigger

What have you noticed? Is there a particular pattern emerging? Try to focus on the category where most of your overspending has occurred, and brainstorm ways that you can cut this back.

BONUS RESOURCE: To help you identify your biggest cause for overspending, download the Women with Cents 7 Day Spending Journal. It is only when you understand the cause of your overspending that you can start taking corrective action to improve your situation: womenwithcents.com.au/wonderwoman

---

STEP 3: Take action

If it is a lack of organisation, try to allow yourself more time to plan your day and get organised ahead of time by meal planning, packing lunches the night before and so on. If you are an emotional spender, try to identify the emotion that is triggering your spending. Are you unhappy at work or in your relationship? Are you stressed about something? By identifying the emotion and the underlying cause, you will be better able to address the problem.

Not everything will be a quick fix, especially when it comes to emotional spending, so try to have a plan for yourself. What are some other ways you can celebrate or cheer yourself up without spending money? Perhaps you could go for a walk with a friend, curl up on the couch with a good book or enjoy a long, hot bath.

So far we have identified your short-, medium- and long-term goals, and have broken these down into weekly, fortnightly or monthly amounts. We have also identified where your money is going and what is driving your impulse shopping.

It's now time to put together a detailed cash flow plan. Often, when people create a budget, it lacks sufficient detail, as they typically forget to factor in certain expenses. This can set you up for failure from the very start, as you haven't put together a realistic and achievable cash flow plan.

So to help you with this task, I have put together a detailed budget organiser, which also allows you to further customise your spending categories and easily track your progress along the way. By doing this, you will have a much clearer idea of where your money is going and where you can afford to cut back in order to make room for your goals.

Q **BONUS RESOURCE:** Claim your free budget organiser at
womenwithcents.com.au/wonderwoman

Automating Your Money

One of the reasons people don't stick to their budget is that they fail to
track their overall progress, often because they believe that budgeting is
too time-consuming. If you go about it the wrong way, it certainly can
be. But there are simple things you can do to automate your money,
which will help you stick to your budget.

Bill smoothing

I used to have fancy spreadsheets forecasting my cash flow (that's my inner accountant shining through!) and I spent hours calculating what bills
were coming in and when, and how much to put aside. Unfortunately,
there were three downsides to this approach:

- It was time-consuming, so I would often forget to do it.

- Because I routinely forgot to update my spreadsheets, I often ended up
  spending the 'extra' cash left over each fortnight, instead of saving it.

- When the bills eventually came in, I didn't have the cash to pay them
  (because I had spent it), which meant I had to rely on my credit card.

And the cycle continued, which meant our savings stayed at zero dollars
and our credit card debt kept climbing. To get back on top of things, I arranged for my bills to be paid evenly each month by direct debit to align
with my pay cycle – this is known as bill smoothing.

These days, you can pay just about everything by direct debit, including utilities, rates and so on. So rather than paying your bills on a quarterly or yearly basis, you arrange to pay them on a fortnightly or monthly basis (depending on how often you get paid). With minimal effort on my part, I was able to avoid bill shock and knew exactly how much money I had left for things like petrol, parking, groceries, clothes and dining out.

Prioritise saving

Human nature dictates that unless you make a conscious effort to save, you will spend everything you have. For this reason, I recommend deciding how much you want to save each pay cycle, and arranging for your employer to automatically pay this amount into an online savings account that you won't touch. As the saying goes, out of sight, out of mind. Using this approach meant that I was actually saving, rather than waiting to save what I had left over at the end of the month (which was always zero!).

> *Do not save what is left after spending.*
> *Spend what is left after saving.*
> WARREN BUFFET

When it comes to how much you need to set aside in your emergency savings fund, three months' worth of living expenses is a good goal to aim for. I typically suggest three months because if you have an income protection policy in place and you are off work for medical reasons, this is generally how long it can take for an income protection claim to pay you (assuming you have a four-week waiting period). Ultimately, how much you need will depend on your personal circumstances. For example, you may need to save more if you work in a role where it could take time to find a replacement job, or if you don't have any income protection insurance.

> **HOT TIP:** Look for opportunities to kick-start your emergency savings fund, like selling items you no longer need, downsizing your car or finding cheaper utility providers.

Swap cash and credit for debit

I've read plenty of articles that tell you to pay for things with cash because you'll spend less. But in my case, what sends me over budget is the five-dollar spend here and the ten-dollar spend there. I have no trouble handing over cash for small items, but I do have trouble remembering how I spent it. 'Yesterday I had fifty dollars in my wallet and now it's gone – but where?'

In a bid to more closely track my spending, I started to pay for most things by EFTPOS – and I mean with a debit card, not a credit card! This way, it's really easy to take a look at my account and track exactly how much I am spending on the little incidentals. Since I now know how much I have left in my account until the next pay day, for me this works just as effectively as having a maximum spend in my wallet.

It's also worth mentioning that we are increasingly moving towards a cashless society, which means that we need to find a way to manage our spending that no longer involves using cold, hard cash.

Isolate your credit card

The final step to sticking to your budget is to remove any ability to overspend – this means leaving the credit card behind.

My credit card came as part of our home loan package, with a whopping $18,000 limit! And, of course, the bank wouldn't let us reduce the limit or close the credit card account because it came with our home loan. To reduce the temptation to use it, I made sure the credit card wasn't linked to any of my other accounts, and then I made a point of leaving it at home. This significantly reduced the chances of me saying something like: 'I'll pop it on the credit card, just this once.'

I have found that using these four simple tactics has meant that I can easily stick to my goals and know where my money is going.

Chapter Summary

Before we move on, it's important to note that budgeting and saving money does not mean you can't have a life. And having a life doesn't mean you can't save. What it involves is redefining what 'having a life' means to you.

If you find yourself always struggling to save, it could be because you are waiting until the end of each pay cycle to save what is left over. Unfortunately, this approach rarely works and most people find themselves living pay cheque to pay cheque, with no savings to fall back on.

The key to saving successfully is to get into the habit of setting aside your savings *first* (also known as paying yourself first), and then mapping out a way to limit your spending to only the remaining amount, without dipping into your savings or whipping out the credit card. This is something I'll discuss in more detail in the next chapter.

CHAPTER THREE

Break Up with Debt

There is an old saying: 'Debt is the slavery of the free.' I believe it has never been more applicable than in today's society. As Australian demographer Bernard Salt put it, we are living it up on borrowed time, and everybody is doing it. But let me quote your mother (and mine) by asking, 'If everybody jumped off a bridge, would you do it too?!'

Why are we so comfortable jumping into bed with credit? And, more to the point, why are we so scared to break up with it? Advertising plays a big role here.

Slogans like 'Because you're worth it' (L'Oreál) and 'Don't leave home without it' (American Express) are all part of a constant ploy to sell you the idea of 'living the dream'. And then there's my favourite – Mastercard's 'priceless' advertisements. For example, one advertisement shows a woman spending nearly $400 on designer clothes just to make her ex-boyfriend jealous. The script is simple: 'New designer outfit: $250. New lipstick: $35. Evening bag: $90. The look on your ex-boyfriend's face: priceless. There are some things money can't buy. For everything else, there's Mastercard.'

Your dream car, dream home, that dream holiday – the marketers are very good at what they do. But there is never any mention of *saving* for your dreams. Instead, the focus is on enjoying yourself now and worrying about the money later!

And the 'dream life' is exaggerated through social media, or the high-light reel, as I like to call it. Other people's dream cars, homes and holidays constantly clutter our newsfeed, adding further pressure for us to keep up. But no one posts the size of their credit card debt or that they're living pay cheque to pay cheque with little to no buffer in between!

There are no posts about the fact that the higher our incomes climb, the higher our debt levels are, when you would think the opposite would be true. What this means is that the impulsive way we spend money can often become a habit, and, as a result, many people find themselves trapped on the debt treadmill. No sooner do they pay a large chunk off the credit card than it has climbed back up by the end of the month. One step forward, two steps back.

In this chapter, I'll show you some simple methods you can use to help you break up with debt, once and for all.

*You cannot get out of debt while living
the same lifestyle that got you there.*

Learning to be a Saver Instead of a Spender

As you go through life, your brain creates new neural pathways as you have different experiences and learn things, so that it can operate more efficiently. What this means for your finances is that when you're trapped in the cycle of credit card debt, over time, a strong neural pathway (essentially a habit) establishes around debt. And each time you use your credit card or you think about your credit card, you are strengthening that connection in the brain, making the habit harder to break.

What scientists have discovered, though, is that all hope is not lost and your brain has the ability to re-train or 'rewire' itself! In order to do this, you need to stop thinking about debt and start thinking about *saving*. In essence, you want to form a new habit.

That's why, if you are struggling with getting out of credit card debt, I recommend saving first and *then* paying off the credit card, rather than the other way around. While, mathematically speaking, it makes sense to pay off the credit card before building up your savings (since the credit card is likely charging you a higher interest rate than you are earning on your savings), if you find yourself struggling to make any progress, then clearly this approach isn't working for you, and it is time to try a different approach.

Experts suggest it takes about twenty-one days of consistent behaviour to form a new habit. So, over a twenty-one-day period, each time you decide *not* to use your credit card, or each time you prioritise *saving* over *spending*, you are strengthening those new neural pathways and forming a new habit.

But to make sure you have really made the change, I suggest giving yourself a longer timeframe. Instead of three weeks, I want you to give yourself a goal of saving for at least three months (or however long it will take you to save up one month's worth of living expenses). And while you do that, keep up with the minimum repayments on your credit card.

Why?

Well, you need some emergency savings, especially while you still have debt. This is because you need to make sure that if you suffer a loss of income, or face any unexpected expenses, you are able to meet your loan repayments and are not putting yourself into even further debt as a result of a temporary setback.

Although I normally suggest my clients have three months of living expenses saved up for emergencies, while you still have credit card debt, let's go for one month first. You can save up the remainder after the credit card is paid off (and any other personal loans). By doing this, not only will you be building up a nice little buffer, you will also be teaching yourself how to be a saver instead of a spender!

CASE STUDY: EMILY'S STORY

I had always wanted to buy my own property without the help of anyone else (particularly a man) in order to maintain some sort of independence. When my long-term relationship fell apart, I walked away with nothing financially and rented my own place – the cheapest one I could find so I could save a deposit for a mortgage.

It took me two years until I had just enough to get into the property market. However, things went downhill financially for me once I bought my house. I had not really registered the dollar amount of extra costs such as insurance, rates and so on, and was still being quite frivolous with my cash.

So I was going backwards. I had a big HECS debt, a mortgage, a car loan and some credit card debts, and realised I really needed to do something. I rented out the two spare rooms in my house, which I really didn't want to do. It didn't seem to make much of a difference, either. I was still struggling to get the debts down, due to not really knowing where my money was going. My family has never really talked about money, so I really had no idea what to do.

Eventually, I joined Women with Cents, did a budget, contacted all of my insurance companies and got better rates, and changed my private health cover. I started putting the rent I was receiving straight onto the credit card debts. I then realised I had two useless insurance policies I had purchased with my car loan, which I was actually paying interest on, so I cancelled them and put the money (approximately $2,000) towards my car loan. I used my tax refunds as additional payments on my mortgage, plus I continued to pay down my other debts.

Ever since then, I have continuously looked at ways to reduce my spending. I've even managed to reduce my groceries bill down to $150 to $200 per month by meal planning, buying in bulk, not always buying premium grade and barely eating out. Rather than buy individual serves of things like yogurt, for example, I buy in bulk and separate into daily serves.

In the past twelve months, I've paid off approximately $10,000 of debt. Now I have no credit card debt, I plan on getting my savings on track over the next six months.

Understanding the Power of Gratitude

These days, it is arguably harder than ever to save money, as, every day, social media and advertising feeds us with the message that we are missing out. Sure, you have a phone, but is it the latest model with a better-quality camera and a faster Internet connection? Yes, you have twenty cocktail dresses, but do they look as good as this one?

I could go on. The constant stream of social media and advertising dictates that there is always something new you should be aiming for. Furthermore, if you don't have it, you are led to believe that you are missing out in a big way.

We've been conditioned to want, want and want some more, and many of us are living beyond our means as a result – taking out loans and paying for things by credit. All too often, our wants are mistaken for needs, and we crave the instant gratification of purchasing items we can't afford, without thinking about the future consequences.

Living in a constant state of 'want' makes it very difficult to save. So, if you are having a hard time saving, try shifting your focus – from all the things you don't have to all the things you *do* have.

Let me give you an example. A few years after I moved to Australia, I finally managed to buy my first car. It cost me $300 (in fact, the annual registration cost me three times more than the car). It was a bright orange, 1976 Volkswagen Golf. Sexy. My friends at the time were in well-paid jobs, with the majority still living at home, driving cars that cost upward of $20,000. Needless to say, pulling up in my little orange VW made me the odd one out. I remember my dad feeling heartbroken, as though he had somehow failed me by being unable to buy me a nicer car.

I, on the other hand, didn't see it that way. Instead of feeling hard done by or jealous of what my friends had, I felt excited and grateful. I had the freedom to go where I wanted, when I wanted, and to me that meant more than power windows and leather seats combined. I could have taken out a $15,000 loan to pay for a brand-new car just like my friends, but instead I chose to be thankful for the car I had, and not let my 'wants' dictate my behaviour or spending habits.

> *Be thankful for what you have; you'll end up having more.*
> *If you concentrate on what you don't have,*
> *you will never, ever have enough.*
> OPRAH

Now it's your turn. Next time you have the urge to shop, instead of thinking about why you need that new car, phone, dress, handbag or whatever it may be, try taking a few minutes each day to stop and feel grateful. To help you do this, I want you to imagine what would happen if you woke up tomorrow morning without a single dollar to your name. You would learn to make do with what you already have, right?

In fact, you would suddenly have a newfound appreciation for the simplest of things, which are so easy to take for granted, particularly in Western society. So, if you want a new car, try to appreciate the one you already have (after all, all you really need is something to get you from A to B). If you want a new dress, try to appreciate that you already have a wardrobe full of clothes. If you want an expensive holiday, try to find a mental escape from reality in the form of a really good book (remember those?).

> **ACTION ITEM: WHAT ARE YOU GRATEFUL FOR?**
> Every day this week, write down three things you are grateful for. Every time you are tempted to spend money, remind yourself of these things, and see how much money you manage to save.

Spending Money Doesn't Equal Happiness

Throughout this chapter, I've talked about the pressure people face to 'buy, buy, buy' as a result of social media and advertising, and the strain it places on our finances as a result. This is particularly evident during the holiday period, with studies finding that Christmas is one of the most stressful times of the year, especially financially. According to MoneySmart, Australians spend an average of $955 over the holiday season, with the average credit card balance sitting at $1,666 after Christmas.

While money is certainly there to be enjoyed, I can't help but feel that we have become overly focused on material things and have forgotten the true meaning of these holidays. Part of being better with our money means learning new habits, and redefining what makes us happy. Christmas (and Mother's Day, Father's Day, Valentine's Day and every other holiday that has now become excessively commercial) is actually about spending time with family. It should not be about how much money you spend.

In a world where everyone's diaries are overflowing with commitments, these holidays should be used as an opportunity to slow down and have fun with each other, and enjoy the company of our friends and family, especially those who we don't get to see very often. Instead, I see so many people feeling depressed or guilty about the fact that they can't afford to shower their kids and other family members with gifts. Or, worse, stressed about how they will be able to afford it.

Having grown up in a country where my father had to spend an entire month's wages just to buy me a pair of jeans, I have a very different point of view. Where I grew up, as children, we all used to get one gift from 'Santa', which was much like the show bags you get here in Australia. It would arrive at my dad's workplace and he would bring it home for me.

That was it. No bikes. No trampolines. No latest gadgets. No second or third gift from mum and dad, and other family members. One show bag. And maybe some socks and undies from grandma. And you know what? We were perfectly happy.

Until I came to Australia, I never associated these holidays with presents. On the contrary, the memories I cherish so dearly are of the family gathered together, eating and drinking all day long, and laughing and playing with my cousins. The aroma in our house from grandma's cooking.

Decorating the tree. It was never about the gifts.

Now I implore you to do the same.

Please, don't buy into the retailers' clever marketing. How much you spend on a gift does not equate to how much you love someone. As tempting as it is to spoil your kids rotten, they only need one toy to get excited about. And it doesn't even have to be expensive. How many times have you seen children happily playing with the box the toy came in, rather than the toy itself?

Children don't need mountains of stuff. This only sets them up for disappointment. Because the expectation is that next year will be just as big or even bigger. How far can you take it? Is it worth working months, or even the whole year, to pay off the debt racked up for one holiday? One day, in fact?

As I said, this is all pressure that has come from advertising and, more recently, social media. By choosing not to shower your children with gifts, they will learn that happiness is not dependent on having 'things'. In my mind, there is no greater gift that you can give them.

Use this time instead to focus on treasuring each other while you can. After all, you never know what tomorrow could bring. The holidays are also a great opportunity to do some volunteer work as a family or to buy gifts for those less fortunate, instead of each other. You don't have to spend a lot to make a real difference in someone's life.

In fact, there is no better feeling than helping someone in need. Research by Volunteering Australia has found that volunteers are happier, healthier and sleep better than those who don't volunteer. And by helping others in need, you will also learn to redefine your meaning of happiness, and not take for granted how fortunate you are.

ACTION ITEM: REDUCE YOUR SPECIAL EVENT EXPENDITURE

STEP 1: Write down all the holidays and celebrations that are coming up over the next twelve months.

STEP 2: Next to each occasion, write down how much you would normally spend (including the gift itself, food, party supplies and so on).

STEP 3: Tally up the total spend.

STEP 4: Brainstorm and write down some different and creative ways that you can make this person feel special. Allocate a new budget for each of these events and tally up the potential saving.

STEP 5: Redirect the newfound savings towards your goals.

Tackling Your Debt Once and For All

Once you have developed some good saving habits, you need a strategy for paying off your personal debts as quickly as possible so that you can start putting money towards your dream life.

The starting point is to first identify all the debts that you have (excluding your mortgage). This includes car loans, personal loans and credit cards. Write down who the lender is, the balance owing, the interest rate and the minimum repayment amount.

The next step is to determine the quickest way to pay these off. You have a few options available to you:

Debt snowball

This involves paying off one personal debt at a time, starting off with the smallest balance first. The theory is that by starting with the smallest debt, your goal will be achieved more quickly, which will, in turn, motivate you to keep going. This process means meeting the minimum repayment on all your debts and directing any extra repayments towards the smallest debt. Once the first debt is paid off, you then redirect the money going towards that debt to the second smallest debt, and so forth, until you have paid all your debts off.

Balance transfer

If you have a small amount of credit card debt, a balance transfer could be a suitable solution. This involves transferring your credit card debt to a different bank (it could be one that you already have a credit card with or you may have to apply for a new credit card with another provider). Balance transfers are usually introductory offers whereby, for a specified period of time, you can pay little to no interest on the debt that has been rolled over. Here are some things to keep in mind:

- After the introductory period has expired, the interest rate will increase (usually to around twenty per cent).

- The reduced interest rate does not apply to new purchases made with that card.

- You cannot roll over debt from personal loans.

- A balance transfer fee (usually one to two per cent) often applies.

HOT TIP: Beware of unintentionally doubling your credit limit. When it comes to balance transfers and debt consolidation, it can take a long time to close down the existing credit card. If you aren't careful, you could double your debt. For example, let's say you have a credit card balance of $5,000 and you've just rolled that over onto a new, interest-free credit card. If your original account remains open, the temptation is there to spend that $5,000 again. This is why, when consolidating debts, it's important to cut up the old credit card, even while you wait for the account to formally close.

Debt consolidation (secured or unsecured personal loan)

If you aren't in a position to use a balance transfer, and having multiple credit card or personal loans is adding to your financial stress and anxiety, then consider debt consolidation. This involves applying for a personal loan which will cover all (or most of) your existing debts. You can choose a timeframe (usually between one and seven years) to pay the loan off, and this can help with reducing the repayment amounts and giving your cash flow a bit of breathing room.

Personal loan interest rates vary depending on the amount of debt, your credit score and risk profile, and whether or not you own a home. The interest rates are usually less than those on credit cards, and can be reduced further by offering an item, such as your car, as security. Keep in mind that if you default on your repayments, it could put your security (in this case, your car) at risk of repossession.

Debt consolidation (mortgage)

If you own your home, you may be able to refinance and consolidate your personal debt into your home loan. The benefit of doing this is that home loan interest rates are significantly lower than those for credit cards and personal loans, so it would enable you to save money and pay your debt off quicker. However, if you are going to do this, you need to make sure you structure your loan appropriately. Otherwise, it could, in fact, end up costing you more in the long run.

Let's say you have a $300,000 mortgage and $40,000 in personal debt that you wish to consolidate (let's say this is made up of a $10,000 credit card debt, a $5,000 personal loan and a $25,000 car loan). If you consolidate these smaller debts into your mortgage and take out a new home loan of $340,000, you will have lost visibility of your personal debts and essentially spread out the repayments over a thirty-year term. Despite the lower interest rate, this is going to cost you more, as you have just taken a short-term debt and spread it out over thirty years.

If you want to make debt consolidation work for you, what you want to do is obtain a $340,000 approval limit for your home loan, and then split this into two or more loan accounts. You could choose to have your mortgage split into two loans (or sub accounts) – $300,000 for your home and $40,000 for your personal debts. Or if you prefer greater visibility, so you can focus on one debt at a time, you could split your mortgage into four loans so you can see each debt separately. Then, rather than stick to the minimum repayments (remember, doing that will mean it takes thirty years to pay these debts off), you want to redirect the amount you are currently paying off onto those debts so that you get the maximum benefit of the lower interest rate and can pay these personal debts off as quickly as possible.

Again, just as with secured personal loans, you need to keep in mind that by consolidating your personal loans into your home loan, it could mean that you are now putting your home at risk in the event that you default on your loan repayments.

HOT TIP: If you are struggling with debt, it might be worth calling the National Debt Helpline at 1800 007 007. Their financial counsellors are experienced at helping clients to navigate their debts and understand the options available. Best of all, it is a free service.

Chapter Summary

Breaking up with debt is no easy feat – especially when we're told to 'buy, buy, buy' on a daily basis. But if we don't break free from debt, the consequences can be dire. Too many of us fail to reflect on our spending habits and understand the impact they have on our finances.

Being better with money means making a conscious effort to eliminate debt. This can be done by learning to be a saver instead of a spender, using the power of gratitude to resist impulse purchases and putting together a plan to pay off existing debt.

Part Two:

Building Your Dream Life

CHAPTER FOUR

Manage Your Mortgage Better to Build Wealth

At this stage, we've covered three of the seven core areas of your financial plan – values and goals, budgeting and debt management. But there's a lot more you need to know about managing debt, particularly when it comes to your mortgage.

Thirty years ago, our biggest household expense was food. These days, it's the cost of housing. According to an Australian Bureau of Statistics Household Expenditure Survey, Australian families spend, on average, 19.6 per cent of their weekly household income on housing (meaning either rent or mortgage payments). With interest rates at historical lows, and the timing of the next rate rise being widely speculated by experts, there has never been a more important time to have a solid plan for managing your mortgage.

It's also not enough to assume that you will automatically build equity in your home without having to make extra repayments. Roy Morgan research shows that 8.9 per cent of mortgage holders in Australia have been identified as having little to no equity in their mortgage, up from eight per cent in the previous twelve months. If house prices continue to fall, the number of mortgage holders with no equity will continue to increase, meaning it's no longer safe to assume that you will automatically build equity in your home.

If you plan correctly, you're more likely to have freedom of choice about what you want to do with your life, and the ability to build wealth and save for retirement. On the other hand, if you don't plan correctly, you may be forced to work long hours in a job you hate in order to make ends meet, sacrificing your health, your family and ultimately your *happiness* along the way.

In this chapter, I'll help you identify your mortgage requirements beforehand, understand the difference between fixed and variable interest, and introduce you to offset accounts. You'll also learn how to pay off your mortgage faster, and how to use the equity in your home to purchase other properties.

Determining Your Loan Requirements

One of the biggest mistakes that people often make is diving head first into a mortgage without having a clear plan. When it comes to determining how much debt we are prepared to take on, we tend to base our decision on how much money the bank is willing to lend us, instead of considering our long-term financial strategy and other factors like:

- How soon do you want to be debt free?

- How much debt could you afford if interest rates rose to, say, eight per cent?

- What sacrifices are (or are you not) willing to make in order to afford a particular home?

One of the most effective ways to build up wealth quickly is to buy the smallest, most modest home you can bear to live in, and to pay it off as quickly as possible. Doing this can free up tens of thousands of dollars each year, and enable you not only to enjoy life more but also to build up wealth more aggressively.

Debt is the slavery of the free.

However, these days, we are so conditioned to instant gratification with regard to everyday purchases that we apply the same expectation to our home. Rather than choosing to wait until a later stage in life to buy our dream home, we buy into the premise of 'I work so hard that I deserve to have my dream home now.' And, just like that, we shoot ourselves in the foot and severely limit our ability to get ahead. Instead, we become a slave to our mortgage.

Imagine, for a moment, what it would mean if you had $50,000, $100,000 or more to invest in other assets instead. This is possible and achievable, providing that you are smart with how you pay off your mortgage.

In order to determine how much debt you're willing to take on, I strongly encourage you to factor in the worst-case scenario. What would life look like for you if your income stayed the same, yet interest rates rose? Would you still be able to service the mortgage? Would you be prepared to make sacrifices in order to meet your mortgage repayments? Answering these questions honestly should help you determine how much debt you're willing and able to take on.

Once you have an idea of how much debt you are willing to take on, you need to consider what features you are looking for in a home loan, based on your situation and what it is you're wanting to achieve. For example, do you want to pay off the mortgage as quickly as possible? Are you planning on taking a career break or going on maternity leave, and need some security in knowing what your repayments will be? Are you likely to sell your home in the next few years? Are you planning on renting out the property, either now or in the future?

Knowing what your plans are for the property will help you to identify what home loan features you need, especially since you don't want to be paying extra for features that you're not going to use. So, stop and have a think about what you might need. Here are some questions to consider:

- Are you wanting to pay more than the minimum and so need to be able to make extra repayments? (If the answer is yes, a variable loan is perhaps better for you than a fixed interest rate loan. More on this in the next section.)

- Do you need set repayments for the foreseeable future? (If so, a fixed rate is worth considering.)

- Do you want a fixed rate, but you're also planning on selling your home in the future and buying another one? (Then perhaps it is worthwhile seeking a portable loan.)

- Do you need an offset account? (An offset account is a transaction account linked to an eligible home or investment loan. It is mainly beneficial from a tax perspective, but used correctly it can also help you pay off your home loan quicker. Don't worry – I'll discuss offset accounts in more detail soon.)

- Are you wanting to consolidate your personal loans and credit cards into your mortgage? (If so, making sure your mortgage can be split into sub accounts can offer greater transparency – more on this later.)

BUYING YOUR FIRST HOME

If you are buying your first home, you may be eligible for some government assistance in the form of the First Home Owner Grant (a cash payment) or a stamp duty concession or a combination of both. The conditions and grant amounts are subject to change and are different in each state. They also vary depending on whether you are buying a new or established property. You can find more information at www.firsthome.gov.au.

The government has also introduced the First Home Super Saver Scheme (FHSSS), which enables eligible first home buyers to save for their deposit in the concessionally taxed superannuation system. If you qualify, this scheme may help you accumulate a larger deposit when compared to saving outside super, as you will benefit from a lower tax rate on your savings and higher earnings than would be possible in a typical savings account.

The government has produced an online estimator you may use to explore the potential benefits of the scheme. It compares making pre-tax super contributions with saving the same amount (less tax at personal rates) in a standard deposit account. The estimator can be found at www.budget.gov.au/estimator/.

Only voluntary contributions you make to super will count towards your FHSSS balance. In other words, personal, salary sacrifice and additional employer contributions, but not compulsory employer contributions. Voluntary contributions are limited to $15,000 per year and a total of $30,000. These contributions also count towards the existing contribution caps.

Withdrawals are capped at $30,000 plus associated earnings. The Australian Taxation Office (ATO) will calculate the associated earnings based on a formula, not the actual earning rate. They will also determine the amount that can be released after allowing for applicable taxes.

You can withdraw from the scheme before you have found a place to buy, but you'll need to buy within twelve months of withdrawing. If not, the ATO may grant a twelve-month extension. If you don't buy within the required timeframe, you can contribute the released amount back into super or keep the money and pay tax equal to twenty per cent of the assessable amount.

You must buy a residential premise with any amount withdrawn using the FHSSS. This includes vacant land if you're planning to build. The premise has to become your home (not an investment property) and you need to occupy it for at least six months after you buy or build it.

Before you start saving, you should:

- Check that your nominated super fund/s will release the money.

- Ask your fund about any fees, charges and insurance implications that may apply.

- Be aware that if you receive FHSSS amounts, it will affect your tax for the year in which you make the request to release. You will receive a payment summary, and you will need to include both the assessable and tax-withheld amounts in your tax return.

When you are ready to receive your FHSSS amounts, you need to apply to the Commissioner of Taxation for a FHSSS determination and a release. You can apply online using your myGov account, which is linked to the ATO.

Three key things to remember are:

- You can only apply for release once.

- Don't sign a contract to purchase or construct your home until after your money has been released, or you may be liable to pay FHSSS tax.

- After the ATO has approved the release, it will take about twenty-five business days for you to receive your money.

Navigating the Changing Lending Environment

There is a lot more to getting a loan than just choosing the bank with the lowest interest rate. According to the Reserve Bank of Australia, there are currently over 250 institutions in Australia that you can potentially turn to for a home loan. This includes banks, building societies, credit unions and finance companies.

Many people make the mistake of assuming that the only things that differentiate these lenders from one another are their products, fees and interest rates. As a result, they use these as the main criteria before applying for a home loan. Unfortunately, this can land them in hot water.

One important factor to consider is their *lending policy*. In other words, what criteria do you need to meet in order to be eligible for a home loan? In recent years – as a result of newly introduced banking regulations and, more recently, the banking royal commission – banks have been tightening their lending criteria, making it harder than ever to get a loan.

Lending policies will differ from institution to institution on a wide range of criteria, including:

Your employment situation

Did you recently change industries? What about moving from a permanent position to contracting? Are you currently on or expecting to go on maternity leave? Do you earn a casual income? Are you self-employed? All of these things can affect your eligibility for a loan.

For example, don't assume that if you just started a casual part-time job that the bank will take that income into account. Some lenders require you to be casually employed in that position for at least twelve months. Some banks will not factor in maternity leave and will only lend to you if you are returning to work within the next two to three months.

Your credit score

When determining your eligibility for a loan, some lenders will take your credit score into consideration. A credit score is a number which indicates to the banks how creditworthy you are (that is, how likely you are to repay the loan). A low credit score means you are regarded as high risk and are, therefore, more likely to have your loan application declined.

There are three main reporting agencies in Australia:

- Illion (previously Dun & Bradstreet https://www.illion.com.au/)
- Experian Australia Credit Services (www.experian.com.au)
- Equifax (www.equifax.com.au)

If you'd like to know your credit score, you are entitled to obtain one free copy of your credit report per year from each of these agencies. You can also receive a free credit report if a loan application was declined in the last three months. You can also go to www.getcreditscore.com.au to get your score for free.

Australia is also in the process of moving towards more comprehensive credit reporting, meaning that lenders will now include more information on your credit report, such as your repayment history, so it is more important than ever to take notice of what's on your credit report.

Type of property

Are you buying a vacant block of land? An apartment? A house? Where is it located? What size is the apartment or block of land? What is the area zoned for? What type of title? These are all factors that come into play. For example, while small apartments are more affordable, they can be harder to obtain finance for. If the development is in an oversupplied area, you may find that some banks will not provide funding for it or may require a larger deposit.

Size of your deposit

Depending on the type of property, lenders can have varying policies regarding the size of the deposit. While some may be willing to lend up to ninety-eight per cent of the property value, others may require a twenty per cent or even thirty per cent deposit. Depending on the circumstances, some lenders may require you to show a history of saving, while others may be able to remove this requirement or take your rental payment history into account.

The First Home Owner Grant

The First Home Owner Grant (FHOG) provides financial assistance to first-time homebuyers. The amount of the grant varies state by state and can involve either a lump-sum cash payment, a discount on stamp duty or a combination of both. Where a cash payment is involved, lenders vary on policy as to whether the grant can be counted towards the deposit.

Your age

If you are over forty years old, some banks require that you take out a shorter loan term or have a documented exit strategy. In other words, how do you plan to pay the loan off before you retire?

Your income

Don't assume that the bank will use all of your income when assessing your ability to afford a loan. Banks differ on their policy when it comes to sources of income such as bonuses, overtime and casual work. If you work as a contractor, run your own business or have investment income, all of these factors can affect how the bank calculates your income for borrowing purposes.

For example, the bank may factor in only a certain amount of overtime or investment income, or may take the average of two years' business income rather than relying on the most recent figures. If you are currently (or soon to be) on maternity leave, be aware that not all banks will factor in your return-to-work salary, due to the risk of mothers extending their unpaid maternity leave.

A stress test of your repayments

Lenders will stress test your income and expenses against higher interest rates to make sure that when rates increase, you can still afford your home loan. The benchmark interest rate used is generally between seven per cent and eight per cent and, as such, there can be a significant difference among lenders as to how much you are able to borrow.

Living expenses

Increasingly, lenders are requiring applicants to declare a detailed breakdown of their living expenses. They will then compare this against their benchmark figure and use the higher of the two. Again, the benchmark figure will vary from lender to lender and this, in turn, can impact your borrowing capacity.

Lenders mortgage insurance

The other thing to consider is whether you need lenders mortgage insurance, or LMI. This is essentially a premium you pay for being deemed high risk, and it applies when you borrow more than eighty per cent of LVR (loan to value ratio). Basically, if you are borrowing over eighty per cent of the value of the property, you will be charged LMI.

Not only does LMI mean that stricter lending criteria will apply to your loan application, it can also be expensive. To give you a hypothetical example, let's say you're borrowing $300,000 at eighty-five per cent LVR. According to Genworth's LMI estimator (one of the leading providers of LMI in Australia), you're looking at a premium of about $3,000. Once you hit ninety per cent, that fee more than doubles. It is important to note that the ninety per cent mark is really where the premiums will skyrocket. Ideally, you want to avoid LMI altogether. But if you really need it, try to at least stay below the ninety per cent mark. Otherwise, your premiums will go up significantly.

To Fix or Not To Fix?

Once you know how much you can borrow, and what features you require for your home loan, your next decision is deciding whether to opt for a fixed or variable interest rate. While many people make this decision based on what they think interest rates will do, there is a lot more to it than the future of interest rates. (Furthermore, there is a lot of luck involved in predicting the future, especially when you are essentially trying to beat the banks at their own game.)

So, let's take a look at some of the pros and cons of fixed and variable interest rates:

The pros and cons of fixed rates

One of the major pros of a fixed rate is that you know what your interest rate is going to be for a set period of time, so that means you'll know how much your repayments are. This makes it easy to manage cash flow and protect yourself against any interest rate rises.

A fixed rate is especially useful while you are on maternity leave, or if you are renting out the property. For investors, there is also a tax advantage with fixed rates as you can choose to pre-pay twelve months of interest in advance and, thereby, bring forward a tax deduction (which is handy if you are trying to offset a particularly large tax bill, possibly due to a capital gain).

The downside of fixed rates is that they typically don't have any offset accounts linked to them, and you are limited in your ability to make extra repayments. This will vary from bank to bank, but, typically, you're looking at up to $6,000 a year in extra repayments. There are also break fees involved, so if you choose to refinance or sell the property before the fixed rate period has expired, you can incur quite a bit in costs when you break that contract, depending on how much time is left on your fixed rate period.

Also, because you've entered into a locked-in contract with the bank, you must pay a certain amount of interest over a certain timeframe, even if the official cash rate falls. If you do opt for a fixed rate, consider paying for a rate lock. This locks in the fixed rate that you have agreed to with the bank and protects you against any rate rises during the time between when you apply for the loan and the date the loan settles (this process can take weeks or sometimes months).

The pros and cons of variable rates

With variable rates, the pros include being able to link your home loan to an offset account (more on this soon), and the ability to make as many extra repayments as you like without incurring further charges. The downside is that your repayments will fluctuate as interest rates change.

Two key tips to remember

Before we move on, there are two key tips I'd like to share. Firstly, if you're really torn between whether to go fixed or variable, you can have a portion of your loan as variable, so that you can access the benefits of any interest rate falls, and a portion of the home loan as fixed, to try and protect yourself – to some extent – if interest rates do go up.

My second tip is about comparison rates. So many people, when they're looking at different home loans, tend to place emphasis on the interest rate that the home loan comes with. A comparison rate is actually an interest rate that includes all additional fees and charges as well. It is there to allow you to compare the true costs of loans with different fee structures. Keep this in mind if you're looking at two loans and trying to decide which one is cheaper.

The Lowdown on Offset Accounts

I've mentioned offset accounts a couple of times now, so let's have a chat about what they are and how they work.

What is an offset account?

An offset is a bank account that is linked to a home loan or an investment property loan. It works like a regular bank account, but any money you have in that account is 'offset' against your loan balance, reducing the interest you pay.

Let's say you have a $300,000 home loan and you have a separate savings account with $5,000 in it. In a typical scenario, if you don't have an offset account, what happens is that the bank is charging you interest on the $300,000 debt, and they are also *paying* you interest on the $5,000 that's sitting in your savings account. You then declare that savings account interest earned in your tax return and pay some amount of tax on that.

With an offset account, your savings account is linked to your home loan. This means you're not actually earning interest on the $5,000 you have in savings, so the bank is not paying you any interest on that, meaning there is no tax payable for you there. Instead, you're saving interest on your home loan – because the bank is only charging you interest on the difference between what is sitting in the offset account and how much you owe on your home loan. In this case, where you have a $300,000 home loan and $5,000 in your savings account, the bank is only charging you interest on $295,000.

One of the main benefits of offset accounts is from a tax perspective. Instead of having to pay tax on the interest rate you're earning on your savings, you can instead use it to reduce the amount of interest you're getting charged on your home loan.

Offset or re-draw?

Arguably, you could also achieve that same effect by putting the money directly into your mortgage and redrawing on it if you need to. This is really where the benefit of offset accounts comes to light. Let's have a look at a scenario where you have $20,000 sitting in an offset account tied to a $300,000 home loan.

Scenario 1:
$20K in offset
account

Scenario 2:
$20K paid into loan

$20,000

Home loan
$300,000

Home loan
$280,000

**Tax
deductible
portion**

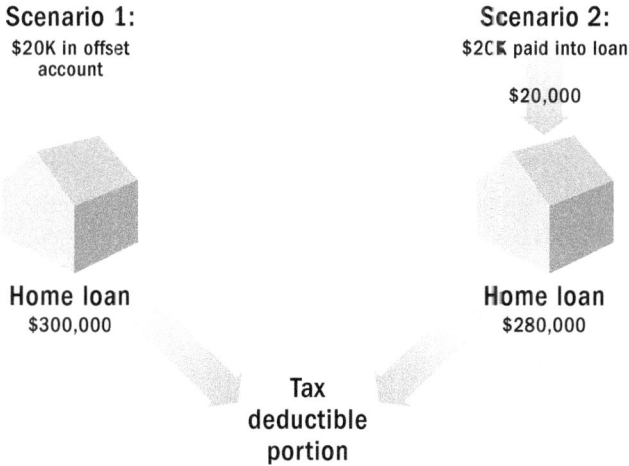

In the second scenario, instead of taking the $20,000 and keeping it in the offset or savings account, you've decided to pay it into your mortgage, thereby reducing the amount that you owe down to $280,000.

Now, let's say you decide to rent out your home and use the $20,000 to go on a holiday. In scenario one, you're taking the money out of the offset account and spending it on your holiday. In scenario two, you are redrawing the $20,000 out of your home loan to use for your holiday.

From a tax perspective, the two scenarios are very different.

In scenario one, you never actually paid down the home loan. Although the $20,000 is reducing the amount of interest you're charged, it never actually reduced the principal that you owed. From that perspective, as far as the Australian Taxation Office is concerned, when you rent out that property, you are entitled to claim interest on the full $300,000 loan.

However, if you went with scenario two and you put the money into the mortgage, and later took it out and used it for a holiday, although the effects on the interest you pay are the same, technically speaking, this is now a different situation to scenario one from a tax perspective. In this case, you have actually gone and repaid $20,000 off your home loan.

And now that you have taken that money back out to use it on your holiday, the purpose for which you're using that money has changed. It is no longer related to the property; it is being used for personal use to go on holiday. In this case, if that's what you have done, when you go and rent out your home, you're only able to claim interest on the $280,000 – not on the full $300,000.

That is basically the difference and the true benefit of using an offset account versus not using it. It really comes down to strategically thinking about what your plans are for that property, and whether you are likely to encounter that scenario. In that case, it may be worthwhile having an offset account as part of your home loan.

Using the offset account to get out of debt quicker

While the primary benefit of offset accounts is from a tax perspective, there is another benefit to using them. Used correctly, an offset account can help you pay off your mortgage quicker. But there's a catch. It requires you to be very disciplined with the use of a credit card, so it is really important to know your money mindset before trying to implement the following strategy.

So, what's the most effective way to set up an offset account?

You may have noticed that offset accounts typically come as part of a package deal. In other words, as part of your mortgage, you will receive an offset account and a credit card, all for a set monthly or annual fee. The reason for the credit card is to help you implement the following system. In short, you want to ensure that any income you receive stays in the offset account as long as possible and, in doing so, reduces the amount of interest you are charged.

CASE STUDY: USING AN OFFSET ACCOUNT
TO SAVE ON HOME LOAN INTEREST

Let's say you have a $300,000 home loan. Linked to this is your offset account, into which you will deposit your salary, rent (if it's for an investment property) and any other income you're earning. You will then use the credit card that you received as part of the package to pay your living expenses and, in doing so, take advantage of the fifty-five-day interest-free period.

Then, as the repayments for the home loan and credit card are due, they will come out of your offset account. Most banks will allow you to set up what's called a sweep. Whatever amount is owing on the credit card will automatically get taken out of the offset account on the due date without you having to worry about it (assuming there is enough money sitting in the offset account).

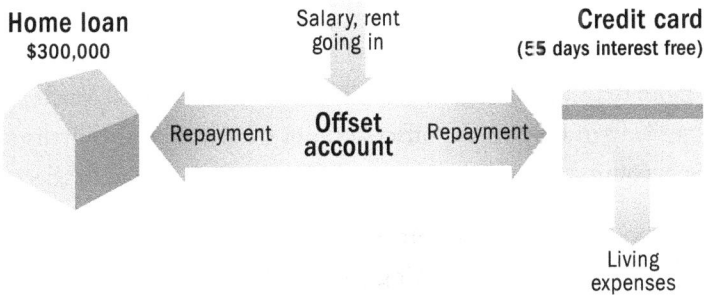

Home loan
$300,000

Salary, rent
going in

Credit card
(55 days interest free)

Repayment **Offset account** Repayment

Living expenses

The idea is to keep as much money as you can in the offset account for as long as possible, so it has the maximum impact with regard to saving you interest on your home loan.

A word of caution

You have to be very careful with this setup, as you can get into the habit of using the credit card without really thinking about what you're doing (the cynic in me will say that this is precisely what the bank wants!). If you end up putting more money on the credit card than you have available, you will start to accumulate credit card debt.

Remember, if you don't pay the full amount that's owing by the end of the fifty-five-day interest-free period, you will lose that interest-free period for the previous month and the month after, and, therefore, this setup will end up costing you money instead of saving you money. This is why it is really important to know your money mindset and whether you are capable of being disciplined with the credit card. If not, then it is best not to attempt this structure until you have a better handle on your spending.

Is it worth the cost?

Unless there is a tax advantage to having an offset account, it is important to consider how you are using the offset account and whether the fees are worth paying. Sometimes the cost of the offset account is actually more than the savings you can achieve. Consider how much money you're likely to have in the offset account or, if you're already using an offset account, take a look at how much money you've had in there.

Take a look at the current interest rate on your home loan and do the maths. Check if the dollar saving you're achieving on your home loan is more than the fee you're paying. For example, if you have $5,000 sitting in your savings account and your interest rate on your home loan is 4.44 per cent, that gives you an annual saving of $220. Now, if your annual fee for the offset account is $395, it may not be worth it (unless, of course, you are wanting the offset account for tax purposes).

I see many people setting up offset accounts without giving it a second thought, but sometimes you can end up paying high fees for something you're not really getting much benefit out of. Make sure you do the numbers to determine whether an offset account really is worthwhile.

The Secret to Becoming Mortgage Free

Before we can start talking about how you're going to pay off your mortgage as quickly as possible, you need to first understand how your loan works and how your repayments are structured.

Let me ask you something. What portion of your monthly repayment do you think goes towards paying down your home loan, and what portion towards interest charges? Many people would probably say half-half. Let's say you have a $500,000 loan, a thirty-year loan term and a 5.2 per cent interest rate. In this case, the monthly repayment is $2,745. Of this, a whopping $2,166 will just go to interest in the first twelve months.

It is important to know that in the first few years of the mortgage, the majority of the repayments (if you're sticking to the minimum repayment amounts) are just going to be eaten away by interest. Let's take a closer look at a hypothetical loan repayment structure (for the loan outlined earlier) to really get an understanding of how this works.

Year	Total payments	Principal reduction (loan amount repaid)
1	$32,947	$7,115
2	$32,947	$7,493
7	$32,947	$9,711
15	$32,947	$14,711
20	$32,947	$19,068
30	$32,947	$32,037

The banks use a very particular formula (known as the Rule of 78) to calculate what your loan repayments are going to be. This formula works in such a way that in the first few years of the loan term, the majority of the repayments are just going towards interest. In a sense, your interest is very frontloaded.

Let's say your annual repayments are $32,947. In year one, only $7,000 is actually going towards the loan itself. Everything else is eaten away by interest. Same goes for year two. You're paying off slightly more in year seven, but it's really not until you start reaching the halfway mark of your loan term that your principal repayments start to be about half of the total repayment amount. It will actually take sixteen years before interest eats up less than half of your repayment, and the total interest paid in this case is an eye-watering $488,400 (almost as much as the original loan amount!).

This example is not designed to scare you or depress you – it is simply to help you understand what happens if you only cover the minimum repayments of your loan. If you do this, particularly in the first few years of the loan term, the majority of your repayments will be eaten away by interest, and you will do little more than just tread water. But fear not. In the next section, we will talk about how to change this scenario so that it works to your advantage.

Now that you have a better understanding of how your home loan works and how repayments are structured, let's start talking about what you can do to pay off the loan faster.

Tip 1: Every little bit counts

Using the same example from the previous section, let's take a look at what would happen if you were to pay an extra fifty dollars a month on top of your minimum repayments. Fifty dollars is not a huge amount of money – I'm sure you could find a way to save an extra fifty dollars a month without having to try very hard.

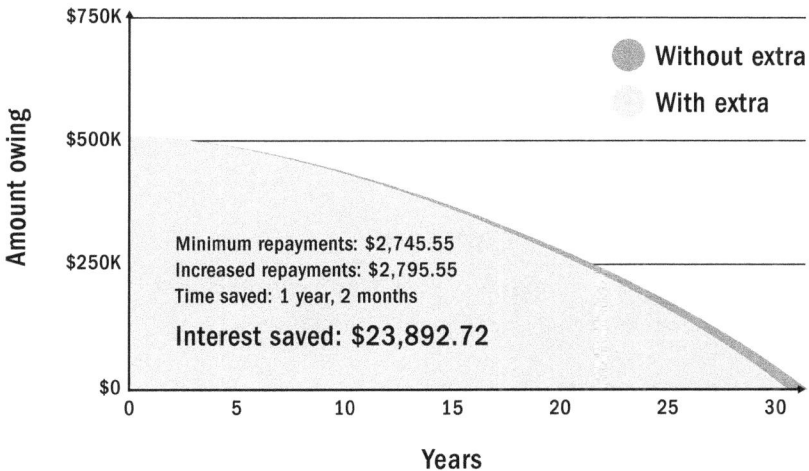

Source: Financial Calculators © VisionAbacus Pty Ltd 2018

If you were to put an extra fifty dollars towards the minimum monthly repayments, you'd be saving almost $24,000 in interest and shaving a little over a year off your mortgage.

You can start to see how just adding small amounts to your minimum repayments can really start to go a long way. So take a look at everyday saving opportunities (like shopping at Aldi rather than Coles – I recently made the switch and saved thirty dollars in my first shop!) and put those savings into your mortgage. Even ten dollars a week can save you thousands, as you've seen in the example I've just shared.

> *A home without equity is just a*
> *rental with debt.*
> MICHAEL LEWIS

Tip 2: Make fortnightly repayments

Another easy tactic is to make fortnightly instead of monthly repayments. Because of the way the payments are structured, you're basically squeezing in one extra repayment each year, and that can start to shave an extra five years off your mortgage.

Tip 3: Don't reduce your repayments

A really easy win is not to reduce your repayments when interest rates fall or if you are refinancing (more on this in the next section).

Tip 4: Prepare for the future

When rates are low, base your repayments on a higher rate (such as seven to eight per cent). This will really start to eat into your mortgage, helping you pay it off as quickly as possible. Now, no one really knows when rates will start to go back up. But the general consensus is that the current level is certainly not sustainable in the long run.

Tip 5: Make the most of your offset account (if you have one)

Going back to offset accounts, if you have one, make sure you're making the most out of it and that you really are using it as much as possible. Make sure you have as much money as possible sitting in that account, and keep it sitting in there for as long as possible.

Go back and do a review as to whether you're getting benefits out of the offset account, whether it is costing you more than it's saving, and whether there's a significant tax advantage. If there isn't, and it's not saving you more than it's costing you, perhaps look at switching to a basic or no-frills product. You can then take that money that you're saving in fees and put it straight into your mortgage.

Tip 6: Avoid the traps

It's important to remember that the banks are in the business of debt. The longer you stay in debt, the more profit the bank makes. Certain features are designed to keep you in debt for longer. These include repayment holidays, interest-only options and a redraw facility. While these are all handy features and nice to have, they're really there as a decoy to keep you in debt for longer, so don't mistake them for a value-add that the bank is offering. Really try to avoid them unless absolutely necessary.

Again, be careful with offset accounts. Banks are very good at what they do, and they devote huge resources to understanding consumer behaviour and designing the products that they offer us. For example, they know that you are more likely to spend money if it's sitting in your offset account than if you put it into your mortgage.

This is ultimately why offset accounts were introduced in the first place. Yes, there is a nifty tax advantage to them, but they're essentially a decoy to distract you from paying off the mortgage. If you are using an offset account, make sure you're getting a tax advantage out of it. If that isn't the case, consider just doing away with the offset account altogether and using a more basic mortgage setup.

The other thing to bear in mind is that the banks like what they refer to as 'sticky clients', as they're more profitable. For this reason, they will offer you as many products as possible. When you get a mortgage, for example, they'll give you a bank account, a credit card, offer you insurance – as many things as they can to make it as hard as possible for you to change banks or refinance. From their perspective, the more products you have, the less likely you are to leave.

To be honest, it is a very effective strategy. I've had a number of conversations with people who know they can get a better deal elsewhere, but they say, 'Oh, but then I have to move my home and contents insurance, and I have to change all of my direct debits over and all of that, and it is too much work so we will stay where we are.' This is where you are really starting to pay what I call the lazy tax.

So, make sure you keep your eyes open and don't be naive. A bank is a business. While it can help you in a number of major ways, its ultimate goal is to make a profit. So, whenever the bank offers you something, ask yourself, 'Is this helping or hindering my efforts to pay off my mortgage?'

In the following case study, Megan reveals how she became mortgage-free by the age of thirty-five.

CASE STUDY: MEGAN'S STORY

Paying off the mortgage was a priority right from the moment we signed on the dotted line. My parents had to sell our home and possessions when I was ten years old, and I've been determined ever since to not have that happen to me and my own family. I bought my first home (with my now husband) when I was twenty and reached the goal of being mortgage-free when I was thirty-five. There were three main strategies that I kept in mind the whole time:

- Always pay more than the minimum.

- Keep a mortgage offset account, so that other savings help to reduce mortgage interest.

- Put any money above your standard salaries (bonuses, tax returns and a portion of all pay rises) into the mortgage.

Now, we get a big buzz when we look around our property and think, 'We *own* this!' No one can take this security away from us. Being mortgage-free also gives my family incredible freedom. My husband and I can spend more time with our kids and we go on fun family holidays. And we've been able to make career changes that have meant pay cuts and unstable pay, based on lifestyle and career dreams, without worrying about whether we can pay the mortgage while doing it.

The Refinancing Mistake That's Costing You Thousands

Refinancing involves paying out your current loan with a new one. One reason to do so would be to access a better deal on your mortgage. Refinancing can be an excellent tool to help you become debt-free quicker. However, in my experience, many borrowers are making a very simple mistake, which means they are actually staying in debt for longer!

In the earlier chapters, I spoke about our money mindset, and the inclination to stick with the status quo or accept the default option. This behaviour is especially common when it comes to the way we manage our home loans. As a mortgage broker, what I see happen most often when a client refinances their home loan is that they take up the standard thirty-year term (again) and they stick with the new minimum repayments.

We spoke earlier about how our mortgage repayments are structured and that in the first half of the loan term, most of our repayments are eaten away by interest. Now, consider the fact that Australian mortgage holders are refinancing more than ever before. A recent report by KPMG found that sixty-one per cent of borrowers were refinancing at least once in a five-year period, with the youngest generation being most likely to refinance, as often as every twelve months.

Now, consider that each time you do this, you stick to the new (lower) minimum repayments. All you are essentially doing is extending your loan term each time and keeping yourself in the perpetual cycle of paying off interest.

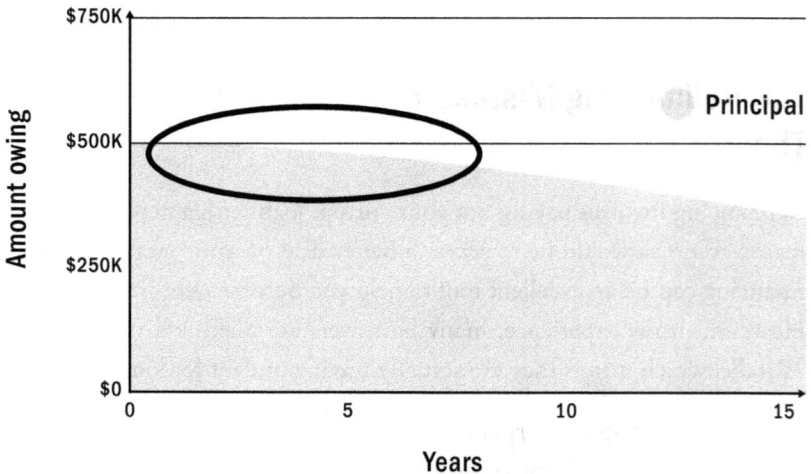

Source: Financial Calculators © VisionAbacus Pty Ltd 2018

I'm not saying you shouldn't refinance. However, the approach you take to refinancing can make the difference between building up equity and forever staying in debt. Let's delve a little deeper to see how all this works and then we'll talk about how to make refinancing work for you.

Let's stick with the same example we've used so far (a $500,000 loan, a 5.2 per cent interest rate and a thirty-year mortgage). So, let's say you're three years in and you've managed to reduce your balance to $477,000. So far, you've paid $76,000 in interest. You can see that there are better offers out there, so you decide to refinance.

Because you've reduced the loan amount to $477,000, that's the amount you'll refinance. You manage to secure an interest rate of 4.8 per cent over a new thirty-year loan term. So, the total interest payable for the second loan (if you stick to it for the remaining thirty years) will be $420,399. This brings the total interest paid over the thirty-three years to $500,738.

Now, if you had stuck with the first loan, even though the interest rate is higher, the total interest payable would have been $488,400. In this case, it is costing you $12,338 to refinance, without factoring in loan exit fees or loan application fees, or anything like that.

As I've said, the point here is not to avoid refinancing altogether. On the contrary, refinancing can be a great way to get a more competitive offer. But in order to get the most out of refinancing, you should maintain the higher repayments that you're already making and take advantage of the fact that you're getting charged at a lower interest rate. If you do this, a larger portion of your repayments will go towards paying off the debt, rather than just the interest.

Let's revisit that same example, but this time let's stick to our original repayments. With a home loan of $500,000 and an interest rate of 5.2 per cent, our minimum monthly repayments are $2,745.55. If, three years in, we refinance the balance of $477,000 to a 4.8 per cent loan, our new minimum monthly repayments are $2,502.65. As we saw earlier, if we stick to these repayments it will cost us a total of $500,738 in interest across both home loans (the original and the refinanced amount).

However, if we stick with our original repayments of $2,745.55, while accessing the lower interest rate, we will reduce the loan term on the refinanced amount down from thirty years to twenty-four years and ten months.

If we tally up the interest payable on the refinanced amount ($339,696) and the interest paid on the original loan ($76,000), we arrive at a total of $415,696, which is a saving of $72,704! So the bottom line is that refinancing is a great tool to help you become debt-free quicker, providing that you pay more than the minimum on your new mortgage.

Using Your Equity to Purchase Another Property

It's no secret that Aussies love property. A very common strategy used to build up an investment portfolio is to utilise equity in properties you already own, in the place of a deposit, when buying a new property. Equity is essentially unrealised profit. It is the difference between the value of the property and the amount you owe to the bank. Let's look at what happens if you want to use the equity in your home to purchase another property.

Let's say you want to purchase an investment property worth $400,000. And let's say your home is also worth $400,000 and you have a mortgage of $280,000. This means you have thirty per cent equity in your home, some of which you can utilise to purchase your next investment. Now, there's actually a couple of ways you can structure your loans, and I'll run you through the pros and cons of each.

Option 1: Redraw

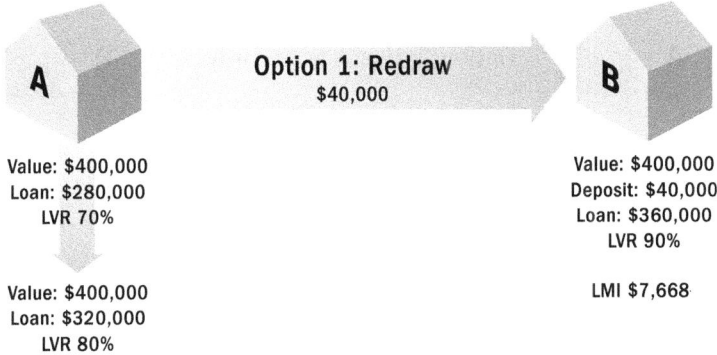

A

Option 1: Redraw
$40,000

B

Value: $400,000
Loan: $280,000
LVR 70%

Value: $400,000
Deposit: $40,000
Loan: $360,000
LVR 90%

Value: $400,000
Loan: $320,000
LVR 80%

LMI $7,668

Let's say you have $40,000 you could redraw, so you could take your loan up to $320,000. This would increase your LVR from seventy per cent to eighty per cent, meaning you would still avoid paying lenders mortgage insurance, and you could put the $40,000 towards a deposit for your next property.

This means the loan for property B would be for $360,000. This property is sitting at ninety per cent LVR, so it has ten per cent equity in it. In this instance, you would be looking at paying around $7,700 in lenders mortgage insurance on property B. Essentially, property A is used as security for loan A and property B is used as security for loan B. If you choose to sell one of them, or if you default on one of them, it does not in any way impact what happens with the second property.

Option 2: Use Property A as Security

Your other option is to take your existing home (property A) and use it as security against property B. In this case, when you purchase property B, it is still worth $400,000, but you're not actually paying any deposit on it. Instead, you're borrowing the full $400,000 by using the equity in property A as security.

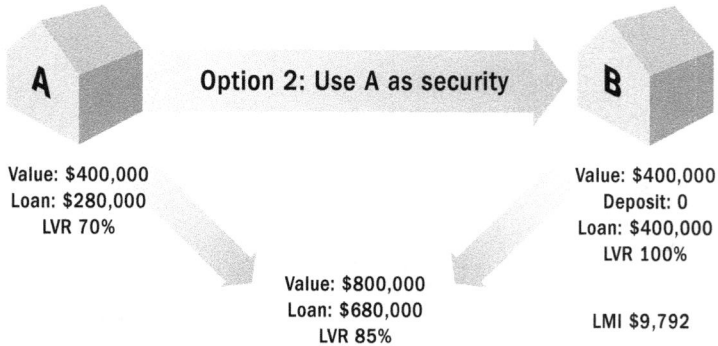

A

Value: $400,000
Loan: $280,000
LVR 70%

Option 2: Use A as security

B

Value: $400,000
Deposit: 0
Loan: $400,000
LVR 100%

Value: $800,000
Loan: $680,000
LVR 85%

LMI $9,792

If you do this, the two properties are linked – and, of course, you're having to pay lenders mortgage insurance. But, in this case, instead of it being based on a loan of $360,000, it is going to be based on the combined debt of the two properties.

In this example, both properties are worth a combined total of $800,000, and the combined debt is $680,000, so collectively you're sitting at an LVR of eighty-five per cent, which means you're paying lenders mortgage insurance of $9,792 (compared to $7,668 in option one). So, with option two, even though you're achieving the same result, you're paying a higher LMI premium.

The other factor to consider in this second scenario is that because the two properties are now linked, if you were to sell property A, you wouldn't be able to keep all of the proceeds from the sale for yourself. You would have to pay down loan B until it reached the eighty per cent LVR mark (or however much the bank requires), so that it could stand in its own right.

Also, if you were to default on loan B, ultimately, the bank has the right to decide which of the two properties you would have to sell in order to pay off the debt. Of course, there are quite a number of steps between defaulting on the loan and getting to the stage where the bank is choosing what you're selling, but it's important to keep in mind nonetheless.

It is even more important if you're using your parents' property as equity and security so that you can enter the property market and purchase your own home. It is important for you to understand – and for your parents to understand – the implications of doing so. Because, in the absolute worst-case scenario, you're potentially risking your parents' home.

ACTION ITEM: REVIEW YOUR HOME LOAN

STEP 1: Write down your current interest rate and repayment amount. How long will it take you to pay off your mortgage? How much interest is that?

STEP 2: Shop around. Are there better offers out there? Take a look online and see what other offers are around. Comparison sites such as mozo.com.au, finder.com.au, ratecity.com.au and canstar.com.au can be useful resources. Make sure you are looking at the comparison rate, not just the interest rate.

BONUS RESOURCE: Check out the Women with Cents website for a handy comparison rate calculator to help you with this task: https://womenwithcents.com.au/calculators/comparison-rate/

STEP 3: If your interest rate is higher than the rates available in the market, contact your bank and ask them to match a competitor's rate. If you are not happy with their response, talk to a mortgage broker to find out if refinancing is an option for you.

STEP 4: Write down how soon you want to be mortgage-free. Use the Women with Cents calculators (https://womenwithcents.com. au/calculators/) to determine how much you need to pay in extra repayments to achieve your goal. If your cash flow doesn't allow for that level of repayment, work out how much in extra repayments you can manage. Remember, even a small amount each week can make a big difference in the long term.

STEP 5: Contact your bank and change your mortgage repayments in accordance with your goal. If you are on a fixed rate, make sure you find out how much in extra repayments you are allowed to make and be careful not to exceed this limit.

Chapter Summary

Your home loan will likely be your largest living expense, yet it is the one most often left on autopilot.

How well you manage your mortgage can make a big difference to how much wealth you are able to accumulate down the track.

Remember, not all banks have the same lending criteria, so an experienced mortgage broker can be a real asset to help you protect your credit score and save you a lot of hassle, especially since more paperwork is required now than ever before. It won't cost you anything, as their services are paid for by way of commission from the bank once your loan has settled.

When interest rates are low, it is easy to become overextended on your mortgage. Regardless of whether you apply for the loan yourself or use a broker, don't take on debt based on what the bank is willing to lend you. Make sure you factor in your future lifestyle goals and cash flow before signing on the dotted line as, ultimately, you are the one who will have to live with the consequences, be they good or bad.

CHAPTER FIVE:

A Beginner's Guide to Investing

Investing is a key component to growing your wealth and building your dream life. Ultimately, the aim of the game is to grow your money at a rate that is at least equal to the rate of inflation so that it's not losing value. Ideally, you want it to be growing faster than that, because that difference between the rate of growth and the rate of inflation is your profit, and this is really how you start to grow your wealth.

When people find out what I do, the first thing they usually ask is, 'Where should I invest my money?' I have some good news and some bad news for you. The bad news is that there is no industry secret when it comes to investing. No silver bullet. No one investment that is guaranteed to make you a millionaire. In fact, with the exception of pure luck, there is no such thing as getting rich quick.

The good news is that you don't need to earn a lot of money to build wealth. And you don't need to be great with numbers either. All you need to do is understand how to apply the basic principles of investing, and that's what this chapter is all about. But before you dip your toes into the investment pool, there are a few things I suggest you do first:

- Pay off any personal loans or credit cards
- Build up your emergency savings
- Get income protection insurance

There really is no point investing your money while you still have personal debt. This is because all investment carries risk, and it is highly unlikely that you will find a risk-free investment that pays you a return higher than the interest you are paying on your personal debts. So, from that point of view, your money is better spent paying these debts off first.

You also want to make sure that you have a backup plan in place by building up an emergency savings buffer and having income protection insurance (more on this in chapter seven). This is because the key to successful investing is to maintain control over when you sell the investments. In an ideal world, you want to buy low and sell high, so the last thing you want is being forced to sell your investment at a loss. Ideally, you want to be in a position to ride out the storm, and this is where having access to emergency savings can come in handy.

Four Asset Classes for You to Consider

Once you are ready to invest, you need to decide where you want to invest your money. In my experience, most beginner investors start off by buying shares in a particular company or buying an investment property. This is actually a very high-risk approach. Instead, what you want to do is spread your investment out over several asset classes. An asset class is essentially a group of investments that share similar traits or behave in a similar manner.

The main asset classes are:

- Cash (for example, putting money in an online savings account)
- Property (this can be further grouped into residential, commercial and industrial)
- Shares (also known as equities or stocks, these can be further divided into Australian and international shares)
- Fixed income (such as government and corporate bonds)

Understanding what to expect from each investment asset class can help you make the right investment decisions for you and your family, based on your specific needs and timeframes. Here's an overview of the main asset classes, and their pros and cons.

Cash

The most obvious pro of cash is that it is highly liquid, meaning it is very easy to access and use. It is also pretty secure – you can't lose money by putting it in a savings account. The downside of cash is what's called inflation risk, which means that your money might not grow as fast as the rate of inflation.

When you keep your money in a savings account or term deposit, you don't really have much capital growth. As it is a low-risk asset class, you don't get a particularly high return on investment. The only income that you get from cash is in the form of interest. At the moment, the interest rate you can get with a savings account is sitting around the two per cent mark, which is not a whole lot.

Property

Australians love property – we are a nation practically built on it. Why do we love it so much? Because it's tangible, it can give you capital growth (growth in value over time) and an income in the form of rent (if you have an investment property), and it's perceived to be less volatile than the share market.

The main downside of property is that it's not liquid. In other words, you can't easily convert property to cash. Also, you can't simply say, 'I need some money, so I'll just go and sell the bathroom.' You have to sell the whole lot. And sometimes it can take you months to sell it.

You also run what's called diversification risk. Diversification means spreading out your risk by investing your money in a number of different assets. With property, because it's so expensive compared to something like shares, it means that more of your money is tied up in one particular investment. This is risky because something may happen to that particular property, or to the property market in general, causing you to lose money. Take, for example, what happened to property prices in Perth, where the end of the mining boom saw property prices fall by up to twenty-five per cent.

Furthermore, if you have an investment property, you run the risk of tenants doing damage to the property or not paying their rent. There are also high entry and exit costs associated with property investment in terms of paying for stamp duty, solicitors and real estate agents, which could add up to tens of thousands of dollars.

Shares

Shares are very popular because you can access capital growth, meaning they can grow in value over time. Along the way, you can also receive income from shares in the way of dividends (in other words, profit distribution). It is very easy to sell a portion of shares as well. For example, if you have a hundred shares in Commonwealth Bank, you could choose to sell ten of those shares – you don't have to sell the whole portion the way you'd need to sell an entire investment property.

You also get what are called franking credits. This means that when you invest in a company in Australia, because that company pays tax in Australia, you get a portion of that tax back by way of franking credits. When you go to lodge your tax return, you will declare the income from that dividend, but you will also get a tax offset for the amount of tax the company has already paid on the income from those dividends.

The downside of shares is that they can be quite volatile. Because they can be bought and sold on a daily basis, the price can jump up and down quite a bit. For that reason, they're seen to be higher risk. If you buy shares in a particular company and that company isn't doing well, ultimately, the value of those shares could go down instead of going up, and you risk losing money that way.

Bonds

Bonds can be a little bit tricky to understand, but they are essentially an investment option whereby you are lending money to a government or a company at an agreed interest rate for a set period of time, and in return you are regularly paid interest and receive your initial investment back at the end of the term. In this way, bonds work in a similar fashion to term deposits. Bonds can also be bought and sold on the share market, if you need to exit the investment early.

Where they do differ to term deposits is that, depending on whom the bond is with, they can range from safe (such as government bonds) to risky (company bonds). Because unlike a term deposit, your money is not protected, so there is a risk that the loan will not be paid back to you. Another risk associated with bonds is that bank interest rates could rise, meaning the value of your bond will fall. On the other hand, if interest rates fall, your bond is worth more as it is paying you interest at a higher rate.

An important thing to remember about bonds is that they shouldn't be confused with investment bonds. Although the names are similar, a bond is an asset class while an investment bond is a tax-effective investment structure (I will discuss investment bonds in chapter eight).

Determining Your Risk Profile

Now that you know what your general options are when it comes to investing your money, there is one last consideration to make before deciding where to put your hard-earned cash: determining your risk profile. It's important to bear in mind that while each investment will offer a different rate of return, it will also carry with it a different level of risk. Usually, the riskier it is, the higher the potential return, but the higher the potential losses as well.

This works in reverse too. For example, if you choose to put your money into a savings account, that is a pretty low-risk option, which means it won't pay as much of a return as, say, shares or property. So, before you invest, it's important to understand your appetite for risk and then plan your investments accordingly. Here are some questions to consider:

- **What is your experience in investing?** If you are just starting out, then you probably want to steer clear of complicated investments such as futures, options and hedge funds, and focus on something simpler to start with, like an index fund.

- **What is your investment timeframe?** How soon you need to access your money will determine what portion of your savings you can afford to invest in something like shares or property.

- **How much money do you want to invest?** Some investments have minimum investment amounts, so the amount you are looking to invest may narrow down your options.

- **How much volatility can you stomach?** For example, how would you respond if your investment dropped in value by twenty per cent? Would you panic and sell straightaway, hold on and ride out the storm, or see it as an opportunity to invest more? In other words, what is your psychology around that particular investment and investing in general? Your appetite for risk will determine which investment options are suitable for you.

> *Risk comes from not knowing*
> *what you're doing.*
> WARREN BUFFET

Ultimately, it is about finding that balance between the amount of risk you are willing to take and the amount of return you are after. This is something a financial adviser can help you with.

In addition to determining your risk tolerance, you also need to think about how much risk you can actually afford to take. You might be happy to invest $5,000, but can you afford to risk losing that much money? Is it part of your emergency savings fund? In that case, you can't really afford to risk it and that money is better kept in something like an online savings account.

For example, I've seen people who, after buying property off the plan, think they can grow their deposit over time, since they've typically got a year or two before settlement. Instead of letting their money sit in a savings account, they decide to invest it in the share market, in the hope of building the deposit faster.

In that scenario, you have to come up with the money in time for settlement, which means you have a specific timeframe. In that case, I would argue that you can't afford to risk that money. Because if the investment doesn't go your way, you don't have the option of waiting until there is a better time to sell. If you have sold out of the investment at a loss, you won't have the necessary funds at the time of settlement, and you could face severe costs and penalties as a result.

MINIMISING YOUR RISK

Regardless of your risk appetite, it is always a good idea to do what you can to minimise risk. This usually involves using a combination of the following two strategies.

DIVERSIFICATION

The first strategy is diversification, which means having several investments. There is no limit to how far you can take diversification. For example, you can decide to invest in a combination of Australian shares, international shares, property and cash.

Within your property investments, you can diversify further by investing in residential property and commercial property, and even further by spreading your property investments out across different locations. The same goes for shares. Let's say you want to buy shares in the Commonwealth Bank (CBA). You could diversify your investment by buying shares in several banks, rather than just CBA, and you could diversify even further by investing in companies in different sectors, rather than just banking.

DOLLAR COST AVERAGING

The second strategy is called dollar cost averaging. While the first question most investors face is: 'What should I invest in?' this is closely followed by: 'Is now the right time to buy?'

In an ideal world, you want to buy low and sell high, but only hindsight will accurately tell you when that time was (even the experts can't always get this right). So, rather than getting paralysed by fear of making the wrong call, the principle of dollar cost averaging says that you should just invest regularly and, overall, this will even out.

So, rather than invest $12,000 in one hit, you could invest $1,000 each month instead.

This means that, at some points in time, if you're investing the same amount on a regular basis, you will have bought shares when they were high in price and a bit expensive for what they are. Whereas, at other times, you will have invested when the share prices were at a low point and you will have, therefore, made a profit.

Factoring in Your Timeframe

In addition to determining how much risk you can afford (and are willing) to take, you need to factor in your timeframe. With regard to shares and property, it is advisable to invest over a long term, primarily to protect you against market downturns.

To illustrate my point, I am going to use Commonwealth Bank (CBA) shares as an example. Let's say you had some money set aside and you were tossing up whether to put the money in a CBA savings account or to buy shares in the bank.

Half year ended	Dividend per share (Australian dollars)	DRP price (Australian dollars)
31/12/2017	$2.00	$75.38
30/06/2017	$2.30	$75.73
31/12/2016	$1.99	$83.21
30/06/2016	$2.22	$72.95
31/12/205	$1.98	$72.68
30/06/2015	$2.22	$74.75
31/12/2014	$1.98	$91.26
30/06/2014	$2.18	$80.39
31/12/2013	$1.83	$75.26
30/06/2013	$2.00	$73.42

This table shows CBA's dividend payment per share over a couple of years (mid 2013 to the end of 2017) and also what the share price was during that time. To keep the maths simple, let's say you bought one CBA share on 30 June 2014. You would have purchased it for eighty dollars and thirty-nine cents. If you held on to it for twelve months, you would have received a dividend of four dollars and twenty cents on that share, so a return of 5.22 per cent.

On the other hand, if you had put the money into a savings account with CBA, you would have only earned around two per cent. In this case, you would have received more money from CBA through dividends than if you had put the money into a savings account.

But what would've happened if you needed the money and sold the CBA share after twelve months? If you had bought it at eighty dollars and thirty-nine cents, and sold a year later, you would have sold it for seventy-four dollars and seventy-five cents, meaning you would have lost five dollars and sixty-four cents, plus the cost of brokerage (buying and selling the share). If you didn't want to lose money, ideally you would have waited until December 2016 before selling (if that was something you wanted to do). And if you had purchased the shares in December 2014 at ninety-one dollars, then you would still be waiting for the share price to bounce back.

> *Remember, your ways of handling money have*
> *to work in good times and bad.*
> DAVE RAMSAY

This is why, when deciding where to invest your money, one of the key considerations is the timeframe you're working to. How likely is it that you are going to need that money in the next few years? If it's very likely, you may actually be worse off investing in shares because it all depends on what's happening with the market at that particular point in time.

And if you find yourself thinking property is a more stable investment, then consider the Canberra property market as an example. Due to an oversupply of apartments, unit prices in Canberra's inner south peaked in 2011 at an average of $530,000 and continued to decline from there. In 2018, they sat at an average price of $480,000, according to Allhomes data.

Now, I am not giving you these examples to scare you off investing, but merely to illustrate why some asset classes are advised to be long-term investments. The way to make money out of an investment is being able to hold on to it until you are making a sufficient profit. Sometimes, this can take a long time. However, if you are unprepared to hang on for the long haul, should you need to, you will be held to ransom by your investments, and potentially lose money in the long term if you are forced to sell at the wrong time.

As I said, this is why it's important to think about your strategy and what timeframe you're thinking of investing over. If it is a short-term timeframe (less than five years), even though there may be greater potential for profit, you may be better off putting that money into a savings account anyway. As the saying goes, a bird in the hand is worth two in the bush.

What's Your Investment Style?

Another important factor to consider is your investment style. In particular, whether you prefer active investing over passive investing, or perhaps a combination of both.

Passive Investing

Passive investing aims to maximise returns over the long term by keeping the amount of buying and selling to a minimum, so as to avoid fees and any potential drag on performance. Passive investing is not aimed at making quick gains, but rather on building slow, steady wealth over time.

When it comes to managed investments, passive investing typically involves tracking a particular index. Indices serve as a benchmark of the performance of a particular asset class (or a subset of that asset class). In other words, investing in the top 200 companies in Australia and not trying to outperform the market or do better than what those companies are doing. If their share prices have gone up five per cent, and you've made a five per cent profit that way, it means leaving it at that and not trying to do any better.

Active Investing

Active investing is highly involved. Unlike passive investors, who invest in a stock when they believe in its potential for long-term growth, active investors typically look at the price movements of their stocks many times a day. With active investing, it's about trying to do better than what the market is doing. So, if the market is achieving a five per cent return, you're trying to make more. The way you do that is by making targeted stock selections.

In the example of the share market, this involves a lot of research and following a bunch of companies, and then trying to predict what the share price of each company is going to do based on a number of factors such as company profits, developments in the industry, any announcements around mergers or new products, and so on. Investors then need to determine the best time to buy and sell shares of that company in order to achieve the maximum profit.

When it comes to managed investments, those that apply an active investing philosophy tend to charge higher fees than those who are passive investors, simply because there is a lot more work involved.

Best of Both Worlds

There is a lot of debate among experts as to which investment style will achieve the best returns in the long term. Passive investing advocates argue that active investing can't consistently achieve higher returns than passive investing, especially after the added cost of active investing is taken into account.

For example, the SPIVA Scorecard, published by financial services company Standard & Poor's, tracks the performance of actively managed funds against their respective benchmarks. The research has found that, as of 30 June 2018, over a five-year period, 68.69 per cent of active managed funds in Australia underperformed the S&P/ASX 200 index (meaning that only a third managed to outperform the index).

Proponents of active investing argue that while it may be hard to beat the benchmark when markets are doing well (in other words, a bull market), during a downturn, active investment can help to minimise losses and maximise gains, as this can be an opportunity either to exit a bad investment in a timely fashion or to buy more investments at bargain prices.

A solution could be to do a bit of both, also known as the core-satellite approach. This means putting passive investments, such as index funds, at the heart of your portfolio, so you know that, at the very least, your investments will be performing in line with what the markets are doing. You can also have some of your money invested in other carefully researched and selected investments that you believe may deliver higher returns than the market index.

Investing Made Simple

Investing can be a complex area to navigate, as there are so many options and factors to consider. It's easy to get overwhelmed and give up on the idea altogether. But I strongly encourage you not to. As women, we have an innate ability to analyse (and sometimes overanalyse). Just think of all the decisions we make when it comes to shopping for clothes!

A lot of first-time investors don't have any idea about what they want from their investment – they just want to grow their money. This is much like going shopping for clothes without having any idea of what you are after. So, first of all, you need to come up with a plan and a shopping list.

A well-organised fashion wardrobe will typically have a few core pieces that are versatile and can be used for several occasions. There's the little black dress (which, with the right accessories, is great for anything from birthday parties to funerals), the smart blazer, a white shirt, pants and jeans. Typically, each of these clothing items are classic in style, and can be worn for many years without needing to be replaced (much like passive investing doesn't involve a lot of buying and selling of investments).

Think of each of these items as an index fund that invests in a particular asset class. So if you are just starting out, a simple thing to do would be to invest in a selection of index funds that track the Australian share market, the international share market, bonds and property (that's right, you don't have to buy an investment property yourself in order to benefit from the market returns!), and leave some money sitting in a high-interest-bearing savings account or in your offset account.

Once you have the essential pieces (index funds), you might choose to add to your wardrobe with a few fashionable items (such as satellite investments) that have the potential to really skyrocket. Although they are trendy now, you will probably replace them in a few years' time (much like active investing involves updating your investments as market conditions change).

But, for now, an index fund is a good starting point. The beauty of starting out with index funds is that they're low cost and, therefore, very accessible. There is not a lot of work involved in running an index fund, so they have low administration fees and you don't need much money to invest in one.

They're also good for diversification. If you want to invest in Australian shares, doing so via an index fund that tracks Australian shares will generally give you exposure to lots of different companies and industries. For example, the top 200 companies listed on the Australian Stock Exchange (the ASX 200) are made up of banks, telcos, mining companies, pharmaceutical companies, energy companies and so on. There are index funds that invest in Australian shares, international shares, bonds, real estate and so on, making it easy to diversify across multiple asset classes.

Returning to the fashion analogy, how much money you spend on each clothing item will depend on your fashion profile, so to speak. Do you have a greater need for formal clothing or something more casual, for example? This is much like determining your investment risk profile – how much of your money will go towards high- or low-risk investments? The process of deciding which pieces you want to buy (asset allocation) and how much to spend on each (your risk profile) is referred to as portfolio construction.

Once you know which pieces you want to buy, and how much you are willing to invest in each, it's time to go shopping! When you buy clothes, you typically have a few options regarding where to buy them from. You could opt for a designer label, you could shop at a department store, or you could choose a small boutique or retail chain. While they all essentially offer clothes (or access to a market index), they tend to go about their business in a slightly different way.

In a similar way, you can invest in a market index through a listed investment company (LIC), an exchange traded fund (ETF) or a retail managed fund. From a purely share price or minimum investment perspective, you could think of them in this way:

- LICs are like the Kmarts and H&Ms of the investment world. You can typically buy shares in a LIC for as little as five to ten dollars. They will probably offer a mix of classic and fashionable pieces, and might have a higher turnover of stock than an ETF.

- ETFs are your mid-range options. Think Portmans, Review and Forever New. Share prices typically range from twenty dollars to $500, depending on investment style. For example, you can buy shares in an ETF that invests in the top 200 companies listed on the ASX for about fifty to 100 dollars.

- Retail managed funds are a more upmarket version of an ETF (which, like that designer dress, you probably don't *really* need). While they both do the same thing, retail managed funds generally have higher fees, and generally have a minimum required investment amount of $5,000 or more to get started.

When you are comparing investment options, it is important that you don't just go by share price or minimum investment amount. Make sure you understand how that investment company or managed fund is going to invest your money. In the case of shares, are they investing only in companies that form part of the ASX 200 or are they also buying shares in other companies listed on the stock exchange?

The easiest way to obtain this information is to visit the website of the Australian Stock Exchange (www.asx.com.au) or research houses such as Morningstar to first find out which investment companies or managed funds are in the market. From there, you can go to the particular fund's website and download their product disclosure statement (PDS), which will tell you more about their investment philosophy and fees.

If you are ready to start investing in shares, and you feel confident enough to invest on your own, you can do so by opening up an online trading account. If you would like professional guidance, I recommend seeing a financial adviser before making any investments.

CASE STUDY: MICHELLE'S STORY

My husband and I were only twenty-five when we bought our first investment property. Working in an accounting firm, it seemed that everyone around me was getting rich by negative gearing, so I couldn't wait until I too could buy an investment property.

It was 2005 and prior to the global financial crisis, which meant that we were able to borrow the full cost of the property, plus enough to pay the stamp duty and legal fees. No savings required! The investment did great, the property was never vacant, and the rent was enough to cover the mortgage repayments and all associated costs, such as body corporate fees and land tax.

In five years, we had made thirty per cent on our investment! We were about to get married and so we decided to sell the property to pay for the wedding, honeymoon and some new furniture for a home. But we committed to buying another investment property to replace the one we sold.

Thinking we were on to a sure thing, we bought another property in the adjacent suburb. Except this time, due to changes in the property market, our investment didn't do as well. It has been eight years and not only have we not made any profit, but we are yet to even recoup our original investment! I now realise what a risky strategy our first investment was.

Since then, we have learned our lesson and the importance of diversification, so we have decided to put our spare cash towards investing in several Vanguard ETFs. It has meant we have been able to continue growing our money while not having to worry if the tenants will pay their rent!

Should You Invest More Now or Later?

Many women make the mistake of not investing early enough. We mistakenly believe that it will require a large sum of cash and so we keep waiting for the day when we have more money at our disposal. This isn't necessarily the best approach, due to something called compounding.

Compounding is essentially the concept of earning interest on top of interest. For example, with an online savings account that pays interest every month, if you're not withdrawing that money, you're earning interest on top of interest. This is in contrast to simple interest, where interest is *not* added to the principal, so there is no compounding. Instead, interest is paid at the end of the investment period as a one-off.

I want to run you through an example that highlights the power of compounding, particularly when it comes to investing.

| | Scenario 1 | | Scenario 2 | |
Age	Invest	Balance	Invest	Balance
1	$5,000	$5,300		$0
2	$5,000	$10,918		$0
3	$5,000	$16,873		$0
4	$5,000	$23,185		$0
5	$5,000	$29,877		$0
6	$5,000	$36,969		$0
7	$5,000	$44,487		$0
8	$5,000	$52,457		$0
9	$5,000	$60,904		$0
10	$5,000	$69,858		$0
11		$74,050	$5,000	$5,300
12		$78,493	$5,000	$10,918
13		$83,202	$5,000	$16,873
14		$88,194	$5,000	$23,185
15		$93,486	$5,000	$29,877
16		$99,095	$5,000	$36,969
17		$105,041	$5,000	$44,487
18		$111,343	$5,000	$52,457
19		$118,024	$5,000	$60,904
20		$125,105	$5,000	$69,858
21		$132,612	$5,000	$79,350
22		$140,568	$5,000	$89,411
23		$149,003	$5,000	$100,075
24		$157,943	$5,000	$111,380
25		$167,419	$5,000	$123,363

Let's say you and your partner are just about to start a family and you want to set some money aside for your kids. Let's take a look at what happens if you start to invest $5,000 every year for the first ten years of your child's life, and then just let that money sit and grow on its own, versus what happens if you wait until they're a little bit older and then look at investing twice as much money over the same timeframe.

Assuming your money makes a six per cent return every single year, what starts to happen? As you can see, time – rather than dollar amounts – is the key here. It's not so much about the dollars but *how early* you start investing those dollars.

In scenario one, you're starting today and you're basically investing $50,000 over a ten-year period. Then you stop and let that money grow on its own. In this case, assuming you're achieving a six per cent return year on year, your child will have around $167,000 by the time they turn twenty-five.

If you compare that with scenario two, where you wait until your child is eleven years old before you start investing, and you invest $5,000 a year until they are twenty-five, you've invested over a longer period of time, and you've invested more money.

In scenario one, you've invested $50,000 over ten years, with your child accumulating a little over $167,000 by age twenty-five. In scenario two, you've invested $75,000 over fifteen years, yet your child will have only accumulated $123,000 by age twenty-five. Even though you've invested more in scenario two, that money had less time to grow than it did in scenario one.

My point here is that you don't have to be rich to invest or to create financial security for your family – you just need to start today. The sooner you start investing, even if it's small amounts, the sooner you will start to grow your money over the long term. Many people fall into the trap of 'I don't have money today, so I'll wait and start investing in five to ten years' time, when the kids are older and out of school.' Hopefully, you now understand why you should start sooner rather than later.

Sticking with the same hypothetical example (an annual rate of return of six per cent), let's have a look at what happens if you invest for eighteen years and then withdraw the money or let it grow.

Annual	Weekly	Age 10	Age 18	Age 30	Age 40
$500	$10	$6,986	$16,380	$32,960	$59,026
$1,000	$19	$13,972	$32,760	$65,920	$118,052
$2,000	$38	$27,943	$65,520	$131,839	$236,104
$3,000	$58	$41,915	$98,280	$197,759	$354,156
$4,000	$77	$55,887	$131,040	$263,678	$472,207
$5,000	$96	$69,858	$163,800	$329,598	$590,259
$10,000	$192	$139,716	$327,600	$659,195	$1,180,519

Starting when your child is born, if you invest ten dollars a week, by the time they're ten that's turned into almost $7,000. By the time they're eighteen it's $16,000, and by the time they're forty it's approaching $60,000. What happens if you invest thirty-eight dollars a week? By the time your child is ten, that money will have grown to almost $28,000. By the time they hit eighteen it'll be $65,000, and in forty years' time it'll be $236,000.

I hope these examples serve as motivation and inspiration for you to start putting some money aside, even if it's just ten dollars a week. The power of compounding means that you *can* start off small. But the sooner you start, the better off you'll be.

Seven Golden Rules of Investing

Investing can be a great way to grow your wealth, as long as you do your research and remain focused on your goals. If you want to maximise your success as an investor, there are some key rules to follow.

1. Never risk money you can't afford to lose

I cannot emphasise this rule enough. It is going to do wonders for your sanity and your stress levels if you follow this rule. What do I mean by this? Well, if you have money sitting in an emergency savings account, for example, it can be very tempting to look at that money and say, 'Would I be better off putting that money in, say, the share market and making higher returns that way?'

But you have to keep in mind that any money in that account is there for emergencies. What happens if you do decide to invest the money, only to be faced with an emergency? What happens if you need to access that money tomorrow or next month, or whatever the case may be, but you've invested it and it isn't doing very well at that particular point in time? This is how you get yourself into a situation where you are at the mercy of your investments, and this is how you can end up losing money rather than making money.

There can be serious consequences if you need to withdraw that money at that particular point in time and it just so happens that the investment isn't performing well. Don't risk money that you can't afford to lose.

2. Set ultra-specific goals

Whenever you invest, stop and give some thought to what you want to achieve with that investment. I see too many people making investments without really giving it much serious thought. This is where you need to stop and be really strategic. Remember, the key to getting ahead financially is about being strategic and specific about what it is you want to achieve.

Do you want a one-off profit or do you want an investment that's going to give you a regular income? Let's say, for example, you are choosing to invest in shares. Deciding whether you want a profit or a regular income will help you narrow down what sort of shares you want to invest in.

If you want a regular income, then you're going to be looking at shares that are paying really good dividends. If you're just seeking a profit, and you want something that's going to help you make a profit sooner rather than later (don't we all!), then you may be focused on shares that perhaps are paying no or little dividends, but ones that you think may go up in value.

The same goes for investing in property. A lot of people go into property investment because of the buzzwords 'negative gearing', which means they go and buy property without really thinking about the areas they're buying in. This is where you need to ask yourself: Do you want to buy in the next boom area and make a profit from the eventual property sale, or are you looking for a property that is going to give you a regular rental income (which potentially pays for the loan costs, maintenance costs and so on)?

By being very specific about what it is you want to achieve, you'll start to narrow down your investment options, which is then going to increase the odds of you achieving what it is you're aiming for.

3. Do your homework

Impulsive decisions can really cost you. So, whenever you decide to invest, make sure that you're doing your research, that you know what you're getting yourself into and why.

It is great to hire experts to give you advice – absolutely! Don't fly blind – know exactly when you need to be getting advice and whom you should be getting your advice from. But even if you do decide to engage experts, you still need to make a judgement about the advice they're giving you. You still need to have done enough research and be informed enough to understand why they're making the recommendations that they are making, and ensure that it makes sense to you and that you're comfortable with it.

Seeking expert advice is one thing, but don't take advice from colleagues or your friends, or make impulsive decisions based on what you hear in the news. Yes, it's good to get different opinions and talk to people. But, at the end of the day, the only person responsible for your financial situation is you.

Some people complain about being taken for a ride or given bad advice. That's unfortunate, but complaining is not going to help you. You are the one who has to live with the decisions you make. You need to make sure that you're happy and comfortable with what you're doing.

This is where doing your research and not being afraid to ask questions is really important. If something isn't making sense to you, don't feel like you're being silly for asking questions. The devil is often in the detail. If something is not making sense to you, keep asking more questions until you are comfortable with what you're being told.

4. Allow a realistic timeframe

Whether you're investing in shares, property or any other type of asset class, remember that they are long-term investments. When I say 'long term', I'm talking five years at an absolute minimum, as it can take time for the markets to recover from a downturn.

This doesn't mean that if the investment has gone well before the end of that five-year period – and you've made a profit in, say, three years' time – that you can't sell early. If you've made a profit and you want to cash in on that, and maybe treat yourself or use some of that profit to reinvest, that's absolutely fine. However, you must be prepared to potentially hold on to an investment for several years before it starts to make a profit.

Let's say you make an investment in property or shares tomorrow, and it goes well in the first year. But, then, maybe in the second year, it starts to go backwards a little bit. Are you willing to hold on to that investment until it turns around again and starts to make you a profit? How long are you willing to give these investments before they actually start to make you good money? This is what I mean when I talk about investment timeframes.

This ties into how much money you're going to invest and whether you're investing money you can't afford to lose. If you need money in a year's time, two years' time or three years' time, stop and think very carefully about whether you can really afford to be investing that money in anything risky, be it in shares, property or something else.

5. Don't rely on past performance

A lot of people buy an investment, such as property, because it has historically done well. That doesn't mean it's guaranteed to continue to do well in the future. Same thing goes if you're buying shares in a particular company or choosing to invest in a managed fund. Maybe those shares or that fund did really well over a certain timeframe, but that doesn't mean they're guaranteed to do really well or be the top performer in the future.

Yes, past performance is helpful as far as helping you do your research on a particular investment. But when it comes to the return you're going to get on that investment in the future, don't think of it as a guarantee.

A lot of people wrongly rely on past performance when choosing to invest in a managed fund (professionally managed investment portfolios). While they do their research and get reports on how various managed funds have performed over the past year, five years and so on, they make the mistake of thinking a particular managed fund was last year's 'winner' or standout. Perhaps this fund achieved an overall return of twenty per cent, while the industry average was only eleven per cent, so you invest with them.

But this is not what you should base your decision on. Instead of chasing last year's winner, you should look for consistency. If you're choosing a managed fund, for example, you want to look at funds that have maintained a consistent performance over a long period of time. Maybe they didn't achieve a return of twenty per cent in a single year – maybe they only achieved a ten per cent return. But if they're returning an average of ten per cent year on year, that's a lot more consistent than twenty per cent in a single year.

That's not to say that the fund with the proven track record won't stuff up. But you're going to have better odds with that fund than the other one, which, despite being last year's 'winner', may not have a consistent track record.

6. Don't forget about tax

It's important to remember that all investments carry tax implications, so it's really important to seek advice, ideally before you go making an investment, to understand how it's all going to work and to factor that into your investment strategy. In the case of shares, the dividend income needs to be declared each year in your tax return, so don't forget about that.

Also, when you sell a share or an investment property, any profit you make is subject to income tax. However, there are rules around how to calculate the level of taxable profit so, again, don't try and do this yourself. There are a lot of ins and outs, and it will all depend on what the asset is, how long you held it for and so on. Again, make sure you get tax advice when you're investing.

You also want to give consideration as to whose name the investment should be in. Should the investment be in your name? Your husband's name? Your kids' names? A family trust? An investment bond? A good tax accountant can help you understand your obligations when it comes to tax, as well as offer guidance on how to invest in the most tax-effective manner.

7. Don't put all your eggs in one basket

Regardless of how much or how little you invest, diversification is key. Diversification will give you maximum control and choice over your money. It will mean that you are less at the mercy of your investments because you have the choice to hang on to an investment or sell.

For example, if you've invested over the long term, and you're now at a point where you want to withdraw some of that money to use, if you have diversified, you now have a choice of which investments you want to sell and which ones you want to hang on to.

Whether you're buying shares, property or something else, the aim of the game is really to reduce your risk and maximise your profit. You will do that by spreading out your investments and not having all your money sitting in the one place.

ACTION ITEM: PLAN YOUR INVESTMENTS

STEP 1: Set some goals and map out a plan. When do you want to start investing? How much do you need to save? Which investments do you need to do more research on? Ask yourself the important questions now to help you set realistic goals.

STEP 2: Once you have decided on your investment strategy, start doing your research. It is great to hire experts, but you still need to have a good understanding of the situation yourself. You can start by subscribing to publications such as *The Australian Financial Review* and the Australian Stock Exchange newsletter, *Investor Update*.

> **STEP 3:** Dip your toes in the investment pool. You can do so by signing up for the ASX's Sharemarket Game, where you can learn how to buy and sell shares without using real money. Practice makes perfect!
>
> **STEP 4:** When you feel ready to start investing real money, open an online trading account (if you plan to buy and sell shares yourself) or book an appointment with a financial adviser.

Chapter Summary

When most investors start out, they typically take a very high-risk approach to investing without even realising it. They buy a parcel of shares or an investment property without doing hardly any research. Straight off the bat and with little to no prior experience, they start off by trying to beat the market and chasing high returns. What's more, they aren't clear on their 'why' or what their overall financial strategy is, meaning they take a scattergun approach to their investments, which can be a recipe for disaster.

The key to successful investing is to first understand the difference between being an investor and a speculator. A speculator relies heavily on chance. A true investor, however, is focused on building wealth in the long run and is interested in maximising their returns while minimising their risk. The most effective way to do this is through diversification and by becoming an informed investor who knows what questions to ask and when it is time to seek professional advice.

CHAPTER SIX:

Create a Super Future

Let's talk super!

In this chapter, I am going to help you understand your super statement, and show you some simple techniques to boost your retirement fund without compromising on your lifestyle now. But, first, allow me to explain why super is so important and why you should be paying attention to it.

For starters, we are living longer. According to the Australian Bureau of Statistics, the average life expectancy for babies born in 2014 to 2016 is eighty for men and eighty-four for women, up from sixty-seven and seventy-four respectively for those born in 1960 to 1962. According to the Association of Superannuation Funds of Australia (ASFA), life expectancy is expected to rise to ninety-one for men and ninety-three for women by 2050. This means that our retirement savings will need to last a long time.

Retirement is a function of income, not age.

Furthermore, you can't rely on the government to support you. As governments change hands, and new budgets are handed down each year, there are increasingly greater restrictions on who can access government pensions. You will need to have less and less money, and become poorer and poorer, before the government is willing to support you. Even if you do access the pension, you'll have to lead a far more modest lifestyle than you may have envisaged for yourself in retirement. Let's take a look at some examples based on the current state of affairs.

ASFA has published the Retirement Standard, a yearly publication designed to help you estimate how much money you might need when you retire, depending on whether you would like to have a modest or a comfortable lifestyle.

According to ASFA, a comfortable lifestyle means being able afford a broad range of recreational activities, some home improvements, the occasional overseas holiday, good clothes and a reasonable car. A modest retirement, on the other hand, would mean struggling to pay bills, taking limited short breaks in Australia, occasionally going out to the movies and driving a cheaper, more basic car.

ASFA has calculated how much income you need to have in retirement in order to live a comfortable lifestyle versus a modest lifestyle. These figures are based on the assumption that you own your home and are in good health. Otherwise, these figures would be higher. (Please note these figures are updated quarterly. The figures in the table are based on ASFA's June 2018 quarter for those aged around sixty-five.)

	Singles (per year)	Couples (per year)
Modest lifestyle	$27,425	$39,442
Comfortable lifestyle	$42,953	$60,604
Maximum age pension	$23,824 ($916.30 per fortnight)	$35,916 ($1,381.40 per fortnight)

Basically, if you look at these estimated figures, and consider the current maximum age pension, you're already looking at a shortfall of roughly $20,000 a year for singles or $25,000 a year for couples if you want to lead a comfortable lifestyle in retirement.

Looking further into the future, I believe the notion of a self-funded retirement will become the norm. According to the Australian Bureau of Statistics, in 2016, fifteen per cent of Australians were aged sixty-five and over – up from just five per cent in 1926 and nine per cent in 1976. This number is expected to grow to twenty-two per cent by 2056 and to twenty-five per cent by 2096.

This means that there is going to be increased pressure on the tax system, which may be unsustainable. Therefore, I believe it's going to come down to us being able to support ourselves. If you are in your twenties or thirties, I urge you to start paying attention to your super now.

While it is important for all Australians to take notice of their super, it is even more so for women. According to ASFA, in 2015 to 2016, average super balances at time of retirement were $270,710 for men and $157,050 for women. In other words, women are currently retiring with forty-two per cent less super than men. Although the gap has narrowed slightly in recent years (down from forty-seven per cent in 2013 to 2014), there are still a number of obstacles that can make it harder for women to catch up – unless we do something about it.

Take, for example, the fact that more women than men take extended time out of the workforce to care for children, and that, upon returning to work, sixty-one per cent of employed mothers with a child aged five or under work part-time, compared to just eight per cent of fathers. When you combine the career break, gender pay gap and reduced working hours, that amounts to quite a bit of catching up that women will have to do! Furthermore, under current legislation, employer super contributions are only compulsory for workers who earn over $450 a month, which puts casual, part-time and low-income earners at a further disadvantage. ASFA estimates that women make up sixty per cent of those who would benefit from the removal of this law.

And while the Family Law ACT 1975 recognises superannuation as a relationship asset, Women's Legal Service Victoria has found that superannuation splitting – in the context of relationship breakdown – is too complex for vulnerable parties to navigate, as it largely relies on the former spouse voluntarily disclosing the details of their super fund.

The good news is that every woman has the power to change these statistics for the better, starting with learning about your options when it comes to super and taking a more active interest.

If you think back to chapter five, where I spoke about compounding, the power of compounding comes with time. It's less about the size of the investments that you are making, and how much money you're putting in, and more around how much time that money has to grow. The sooner you start investing, the better off you're going to be come retirement. The same rule applies to your super. Instead of worrying about it in your forties, fifties and sixties, make it a priority now.

In this chapter, I'll show you how super works and reveal how much super you need in order to retire comfortably. I'll also explain the difference between binding and non-binding nominations, share some tips on finding lost super and discuss how to be more involved in your super in general.

Understanding Your Super Statement

Before we discuss how much money you need to retire comfortably, let's delve a little bit deeper into how super works and some of the terminology associated with it. Superannuation is a tax-effective way of saving for your retirement. It is primarily funded by your employer, although you can choose to make additional contributions.

There are laws in place that govern super funds. In particular, the Superannuation Industry Supervision Act, or SIS Act. If you're earning over $450 a month, by law, your employer has to pay a minimum of nine and a half per cent of your salary into a complying super fund. There are plans in place for that level of contribution to increase to twelve per cent by 2025.

Basically, you and your employer pay money into your super fund. The super fund then invests that money on your behalf. When you retire, you then withdraw that money from your super, either as a lump sum or as an income stream (in the form of a pension).

There are specific rules regarding how much you can contribute to your super account and how the earnings are taxed.

Concessional and Non-Concessional Contributions

The money you contribute to super is divided into two broad categories: concessional contributions and non-concessional contributions.

Any money that your employer pays into your super fund (your super guarantee contribution), and any money that you contribute before tax (such as salary sacrifice), is called a concessional contribution. At present, there's a $25,000 annual cap for everyone, regardless of age. This means that if you contribute over $25,000 a year in concessional contributions, then those amounts are taxed at a higher rate, thereby removing any tax benefit of investing through super.

Any contributions that you make into super from your after-tax income, and any government co-contributions that you receive into super, are called non-concessional contributions. At present, there's a $100,000 annual cap applied to those amounts.

The main reason why these amounts are grouped into different categories is for tax reasons. With non-concessional contributions, there's no tax applied to them when you put that money into your super account. This is because you have already paid income tax on that money, so the government is not going to penalise you and tax you twice when you go and put that money into super. Non-concessional contributions have no tax payable when you put them into super.

Concessional contributions and any earnings on your investments in super (for example, dividend income and interest) are currently taxed at fifteen per cent. This is because when your employer contributes money into your super fund, or when you salary sacrifice into super, you haven't paid any income tax on that money at that stage, and so it's then taxed within the super fund at fifteen per cent.

Again, it's very important to keep in mind that these rules change, sometimes year on year, so it's very important to stay informed about super regulations. You can do this by visiting the ATO website or the Australian Securities and Investments Commission's MoneySmart website (moneysmart.gov.au). I also encourage you to seek professional advice if you are thinking of contributing more into super.

Binding and Non-Binding Nominations

Most people don't pay attention to binding nominations until it's too late. Essentially, a binding nomination determines who will inherit your super when you die. 'But I have a will,' I hear you say. Well, that doesn't matter. You still need to make a binding nomination in your super. This is because your super does not form part of your estate. We will discuss the importance of binding nominations in more detail in chapter eight.

How Much Super Do You Need?

We have spoken about how much income you need in retirement, so let's now take a look at how this translates to your super balance. In other words, how much do you need to have in super in order to be able to retire comfortably? Once again, I've attained some figures from ASFA, showing the estimated lump sums you'll need in retirement (assuming you can access either a full or part age pension).

	Singles	Couples
Modest lifestyle	$70,000	$70,000
Comfortable lifestyle	$545,000	$640,000

According to ASFA, if you are nearing retirement and would like to lead a modest lifestyle in retirement, you'll only need about $70,000, as you'll be relying predominantly on the age pension (the figure is the same for singles and couples due to the impact of the age pension). If, on the other hand, you want to enjoy retirement a bit more and lead a comfortable lifestyle, then you need a far greater balance in super – $545,000 if you're single and $640,000 for a couple.

If we have a look at the Australian Bureau of Statistics' latest figures on the average super balances for men and women come retirement age, let's see how they compare to what our actual needs are. For women, the average super balance is about $138,000 at retirement time, while, for men, it's $292,000. This means the majority of Australians don't have enough money to lead a comfortable lifestyle in retirement. Also, you'll notice that women have about half the super balance of men, which is a really sobering thought in itself.

The reason women tend to have a lower super balance is primarily because of their decision to have children – women tend to take a lot more time out of the workforce than men to have kids. And even when they return to work, they often work in casual or part-time jobs (making it easier to juggle parenting responsibilities), which also slows down their ability to accumulate super.

As I said earlier, for anyone in their twenties or thirties, it's highly likely that, in forty years' time, you'll be expected to self-fund your retirement. That's why it's so important to grow your super account as much as you can. While these figures may sound daunting, try not to feel disheartened. Later, I'll show you several ways you can easily boost your super, regardless of your income! But, first, let's discuss some ways to take a more active role in your super.

Four Ways to Get More Involved in Your Super

There has never been a more important time to take an active role in growing your super, and this is especially true for women. So, let's talk about how you can get more involved with your super. Here are four ways to get started.

1. Consolidate your super

Hopefully, by now, I have drummed into you the importance of super and looking after your super. Let's now look at how you can investigate whether you have any lost super and how you can find it.

It's very important to see if you have any additional super lying around. Sometimes, you might be surprised to discover that you do. Perhaps you had a part-time job during your university days that you completely forgot about, and there's a small super balance sitting in an industry super fund. It's definitely worthwhile tracking that down.

When it comes to finding lost super, you actually have a couple of options available to you.

The first option is to use your myGov account (at mygov.com.au) and link that to the Australian Tax Office, which will help you find any lost super.

The second option is to contact your super fund and ask them to do a search for lost super on your behalf. If you have a few super funds, consolidating your super into a single fund can mean you're not losing money paying multiple administration fees.

But before you go consolidating your super, please do a full review of your life insurance (which we'll discuss at length in chapter seven). If you haven't taken out a retail policy, and you've decided that you want to, make sure you apply for those policies – and you have all of those insurances in place – *before* you consolidate your super. Because when you consolidate your super, any life insurance you had in those super accounts is going to be cancelled. In the meantime, if you haven't taken out a new policy to replace that cover, you may find yourself without any insurance.

This is particularly important if you have developed a medical condition (or symptoms of a medical condition), which the new insurance policy isn't going to cover you for. You may even be declined for cover altogether. This is where a financial adviser can really help you, as they can see if it's worthwhile or important for you to keep those super funds in place, just to preserve the insurances you have.

I've had cases where clients have gone to a chiropractor or an acupuncturist for something preventative, but their insurance company has taken this as a sign of a pre-existing medical condition and their cover has been affected as a result. Life insurance is a far more complex beast than many people realise. So, before you go closing a super account, make sure you have read chapter seven and do a full review of all of your insurance.

You should also make sure you understand how much cover you need, and check that you have the right types and levels of cover. If you don't, book an appointment with a financial adviser and get their help in fixing all this up – *before* you go consolidating your super.

2. Check your super statement regularly

Make sure that you check your statement regularly – don't just put it in the pile of unopened mail to deal with at some other point in time. Make sure that you're opening it regularly and checking that the information is accurate, and that you're receiving all of your contributions. If you have made voluntary contributions, or if you're salary sacrificing into super, you want to make sure no errors have been made along the way and that the money is actually in your account.

Remember, this is *your* money. Far too many people make the mistake of thinking it's not their money because they feel like they don't have control over it or that it's not really going to affect them until it's time to retire. That's a huge, huge mistake.

If your employer is responsible for paying super guarantee contributions on your behalf, don't just assume that it's automatically happening. Go and open your last statement, and check to see if your employer is regularly making contributions into your super fund. Are they contributing the right amount? Go back through your payslips and do a crosscheck and make sure that the money is in there.

You may assume the money is going in, but there could be any number of things preventing the money from reaching your super fund. Like what? Well, you could be working for a small business and maybe they don't realise that they need to be paying money into your super – maybe they're not aware of their obligations in this regard.

Maybe they have cash flow issues and they haven't been able to pay money into your super. Maybe they're doing all the right things, but they have opened up another super fund and you didn't realise that the money is sitting somewhere else. Or there's been an administrative error somewhere along the way and the money is being contributed into someone else's fund. Any number of things could happen. Again, it's your money, so make sure that it's there. Don't fall into the trap of thinking that retirement is a long way off and that you don't have to worry about it now.

3. Pay attention to your investments

Did you know that you have a say in how super is invested? In fact, most super funds offer a range of different investment options you can choose from. Each option consists of a different mix of investments, and offers a different return and a different rate of risk (refer back to chapter five where we discuss asset allocation and risk profiles in more detail).

When you're choosing how to invest your money in super, don't just chase the lowest fees or the highest returns. You want to factor in your age, how long you have before you retire (this is your investment timeframe), how much risk you're willing to take on, and how different investment mixes and choices can impact the amount of money you have to retire on.

As you get closer to retirement, it may be worth changing your investment mix so that you're taking on less risk. During the global financial crisis, a lot of people got into a lot of trouble because the majority of their super was invested in high-risk assets such as shares and property. When the GFC happened, the value of their super absolutely plummeted.

For this reason, as you are approaching retirement, you want to make sure that you have enough time to ride out any fluctuations and falls in the market. As you near retirement, you may consider investing your super in a more conservative manner, so that when you do retire, your money is there for you. Whatever you do, make sure that you're keeping an eye on your super and how it is invested, and be sure to take advantage of the options available to you.

To help you understand the potential implications of different investment options, there are a couple of great online tools you can have a play with. The Australian Securities and Investments Commission (ASIC) MoneySmart website (moneysmart.gov.au) and the AMP super simulator (a quick Google search should bring it up) are great if you want to see the potential effects of different investment options on your retirement funds. Please understand that I'm not making a recommendation to invest or not invest in AMP. I'm simply saying that the super simulator allows you to have a play with your super figures.

If you are really hands-on with investing, you may consider setting up a self-managed super fund (SMSF). However, ASIC recommends that you have at least $200,000 in super before you set one up. This is mainly because there's a lot of work involved. There are also a lot of fees involved, including auditor fees, accountant fees and so on, which could outweigh any benefits to having an SMSF.

For this reason, some super funds have started to offer what they refer to as a direct investment option. This allows you to choose specific shares, and choose what you want your money invested in, rather than the super fund making all the decisions on your behalf. So, if you want to be more hands-on with your super, without the exorbitant costs associated with SMSFs, you can consider going down that track. Super funds that are offering this direct investment option include AustralianSuper, Hostplus and ING.

4. Minimise your fees

Once you have decided how you want your money invested, it is worthwhile doing some research to see how your fund compares with others from a fee perspective. Keep in mind that one fund's definition of 'balanced' could be another fund's definition of 'high growth', so be sure to look at the underlying investment split first and then compare fees for the delivery of the same service.

There has been a lot of debate regarding whether industry or retail (bank-owned) super funds are better. Regarding investment performance, research suggests that industry funds perform just as well as, if not better than, retail super funds. This then makes it a question of fees, and retail funds tend to be more expensive than industry funds. Fees for managed investments can vary from 0.19 per cent to 2.5 per cent, depending on the investment mix.

CASE STUDY: NATALIE'S STORY

After spending a lot of time in my twenties and thirties working overseas, I realised my super was lacking contributions and fees had begun to eat away at my balance. At that time, the government offered a co-contribution and I took advantage of that to assist with topping up my super.

By my late thirties, my partner and I were planning to have a baby and I could see that my super would once again take a hit from time out of the workforce. I also learned more about the importance of compound interest and that saving extra small amounts early in my life would add up substantially over time. I wish this had been drilled into me at twenty!

I did some calculations and worked out that by salary sacrificing a certain amount, it would only end up being a small amount less in my take-home pay. As I found I wasn't missing this small amount, I bumped up my pre-tax salary sacrifice contributions to approximately five per cent, on top of my employer's 9.5 per cent.

I'm now in my early forties with a preschooler and have been working part-time since going back to work. I've maintained the additional super contributions of five per cent to help counteract my lower salary while I'm working part-time. I don't see it as cutting back on some-thing else to make room for the extra super contributions – I see it as an important long-term strategy to support my retirement. As it is pre-tax and automatic, you don't really notice the missing dollars.

I am currently investigating changing to a fund that invests more responsibly (avoiding fossil fuels, weapons and so on) and want to feel that my money is supporting a better world for my kids to live in. If I continue with this strategy (and the current super rules remain in place), I estimate I will have at least twenty-five per cent more super at age sixty-five than if I didn't salary sacrifice at all.

Six Factors that Could Help You Boost Your Super

Let's take a look at a few simple ways you can boost your super balance. The first step is to decide how much you want to contribute and the next step is to figure out the most effective way to do it. Here are a few things to consider. (Please note that these figures apply to the 2018 to 2019 financial year and may change in the future.)

Are you a stay-at-home mum?

It is not uncommon for women to stay at home to look after the kids, espe-cially when you consider the cost of childcare. A KPMG report found that for a couple earning the minimum wage, if the mother works more than three days a week, she is effectively working for just two dollars and fifty cents an hour on the additional days. Couple that with the fact that women tend to earn less than men and it is easy to see why, in so many families, it is the working mum who decides to stay at home. Mathematically, this makes more sense, at least in the short term. However, in among these discussions at home, the impact of lost super and career progression is often forgotten.

To make sure that you are truly working together as a team, a simple solution here would be to arrange for contribution splitting in order to evenly divide the working spouse's super between both super accounts (check whether your super fund allows it and if there are any fees involved).

Contribution splitting involves splitting up to eighty-five per cent of your (or, in this case, your spouse's) before-tax super contributions (also known as concessional contributions). This includes any amounts they salary sacrifice and their employer superannuation guarantee contributions. It is important to note that any contributions they split with you will count towards their concessional contributions cap of $25,000 (but not yours).

You may be wondering what the point of this is. After all, if you separate or get a divorce, you could theoretically split your super anyway. While this is possible, there can be significant legal fees involved, and it all depends on how amicable the split is, as you will require your ex-partner's honesty and cooperation. The easier, safer and more cost-effective approach would be to split your super contributions with each other now, while you both like each other and are on the same page!

Do you earn between $37,697 and $52,697?

If you do, and you make a non-concessional (after-tax) super contribution, you may be eligible for a matching contribution from the government of fifty cents for every dollar you contribute. The maximum contribution of $500 is available if you contribute $1,000 to your super and earn under $37,697. This progressively reduces as your income increases. Be aware that earnings include assessable income, reportable fringe benefits and reportable employer super contributions. Other conditions also apply, so make sure you get professional advice or contact the ATO to make sure you are eligible.

It doesn't matter whether you make one payment or several contributions during the year. To receive the co-contribution, you just need to lodge your tax return and make sure your super fund has your Tax File Number (TFN) on record. The government will then automatically calculate what you are entitled to and pay the co-contribution directly into your fund.

Are you in a relationship and earning under $37,000?

If your spouse makes an after-tax contribution into your super, they may qualify for a tax offset up to $540. Your spouse may be able to get the full offset if they contribute $3,000 and you earn $37,000 or less per annum (including your assessable income, reportable fringe benefits and reportable employer super contributions). A lower tax offset may be available if they contribute less than $3,000, or you earn between $37,001 and $39,999 per annum.

Do you earn over $37,000?

If you don't qualify for the government co-contribution and spouse tax offset, it's probably more tax-effective to contribute to your super via a salary sacrifice agreement or by claiming a tax deduction. Salary sacrificing (or salary packaging) is essentially agreeing with your employer to be remunerated in another way other than cash. The benefit received in lieu of cash is called a fringe benefit and, depending on the nature of the benefit, a fringe benefit tax may be payable.

Superannuation is one of the few items that you can salary package which is exempt from fringe benefit tax. Given that concessional contributions to super are taxed at fifteen per cent, for many people this can make salary sacrificing a tax-effective way of boosting their super.

Let's take a look at how this might work. Let's say you earn a $90,000 salary, on top of which your employer pays 9.5 per cent SGC, and you have decided you wish to contribute an extra $10,000 a year into super.

Example: Extra $10k into super

	Scenario 1 After tax contribution	Scenario 2 Before tax contribution
Gross salary	$90,000	$90,000
Salary sacrifice		$11,765
Taxable income	$90,000	$78,235
Less: Income tax	$22,067	$18,008
Less: After tax contribution	$10,000	
Disposable income:	$57,933	$60,227
Tax benefit gained:		$2,294

If you make the contribution after tax, your taxable income is $90,000, on which you will pay $22,067 in income tax and the Medicare levy. This gives you a disposable income of $67,933 and a net amount of $57,933 after you contribute to super. As a result, your super balance will be increased by $10,000.

On the other hand, you could choose to salary sacrifice $11,765 into super ($10,000 into super plus an additional fifteen per cent to make up for the tax payable on the concessional contribution). In this case, your taxable income is $78,235, on which you will pay $18,008 in income tax and the Medicare levy. This gives you a disposable income of $60,227. As you can see, in both cases, you have boosted your super by $10,000. But in the second scenario, your disposable income is higher by $2,294.

Before you do this, just make sure that the value of your employer's SGC (super guarantee charge), plus your salary sacrifice contributions, don't put you over the $25,000 cap. If they do, some or all of your extra contributions will be better off made in after-tax dollars (as a non-concessional contribution).

To start a salary sacrifice arrangement, contact your employer's payroll department. Alternatively, you can choose to make concessional contributions yourself and claim these on your tax return. In this case, you will need to contact your super fund before making any contributions and they will advise you of what steps you need to take.

Do you have a super balance of less than $500,000?

If you have a super balance of less than $500,000, you will be able to accrue the unused balance of your concessional contribution cap towards the following year on a five-year rolling basis. In other words, your cap for the following year is increased by any unused amount from previous years. This can be particularly useful if you have taken a career break and want to increase your super contributions in the short term to catch up.

Are you approaching retirement?

If you are approaching retirement, I would strongly suggest you obtain professional advice, as there are several options available to maximise your super and minimise tax. These include:

- **Downsizer contributions.** If you are sixty-five or older, you may be able to use the proceeds from the sale of your primary residence to contribute up to $300,000 per person or $600,000 per couple into super – without this amount counting towards the concessional (pre-tax) or non-concessional (post-tax) contribution caps.

- **The NCC bring-forward cap.** The annual non-concessional contribution (NCC) cap is currently $100,000. But if you are under age
  sixty-five, you may be able to trigger the bring-forward rule to make
  larger contributions.

  The bring-forward rule allows you to bring forward up to an additional two years' worth of non-concessional contributions and add
  it to the current year's cap. If eligible, you may be able to contribute
  up to $300,000 over the three-year period. The total bring-forward
  amount you're able to trigger will reduce if your total superannuation
  savings are at least equal to $1.4 million at the end of the financial
  year in which you trigger the bring-forward rule.

  The bring-forward rule is automatically triggered if you're eligible and
  make non-concessional contributions in a financial year that exceed
  your annual non-concessional limit. Once triggered, your non-concessional contribution cap will not be indexed for the next two years.
  In addition, you must have total superannuation savings of less than
  $1.6 million at the end of the financial year to be eligible to make any
  non-concessional contributions in the following years.

- **Transition to retirement.** If you are aged between fifty-five and sixty,
  there are strategies available to help you minimise tax and maximise
  your super balance by starting to withdraw some of your super and
  then re-contributing money back in. This strategy enables you to reduce your tax payable now, as well as affecting the tax treatment of any
  super inherited by family members as part of a deceased estate. Once
  again, this is a complicated area so it is best to seek professional advice.

Could Refinancing Your Home Loan Boost Your Super?

If you have a mortgage, this is one strategy I am particularly excited about, as you have the potential to get ahead on your mortgage and boost your super *without affecting your cash flow*. In the previous chapter, I showed you how refinancing can pay off your mortgage quicker. You can also use this same approach to boost your super at the same time.

Let's assume you have a $500,000 mortgage at an interest rate of four per cent. Your monthly repayments are $2,387, with total interest payable over the thirty-year loan term (assuming, for simplicity's sake, that rates don't change) of $359,348.

Let's say you are three years into your loan term and you decided to re-finance to a lower rate of 3.7 per cent. Your loan balance has fallen from $500,000 to $472,494. If you refinance this amount at 3.7 per cent, your minimum monthly repayments are now $2,174 – a saving of $213 a month. Because you are a savvy Wonder Woman, you decide to use this saving to pay an extra $100 a month on your mortgage and also put $100 a month into your super as an after-tax contribution. With the remaining thirteen dollars, you decide to treat yourself to coffee and cake at your favourite patisserie once a month.

Let's say you are thirty-five years old, earn $60,000 a year and have a super balance of $40,000. If you do nothing to boost your super account, and keep working to age sixty-seven, your estimated super balance at re-tirement is $243,419. If, on the other hand, you start contributing $100 a month in after-tax contributions, your estimated super balance in retire-ment jumps to $284,732, which is an extra $41,313 in super! Not only that, but you'll save thousands of dollars in interest on your mortgage.

ACTION ITEM: SUPERCHARGE YOUR FUTURE

STEP 1: Open your most recent super statement and get familiar with it. How much super do you have? Has your employer been making regular contributions to your account (and are they the correct amounts)? How is your super invested? Do you have insurance?

STEP 2: Go online and have a play with some super calculators and compare their results. Roughly how much money are you likely to have in retirement?

STEP 3: Do a quick budget calculation. How much income are you likely to need when you retire? Are you on track for achieving that result?

STEP 4: Consider making extra contributions to super. The Super Guru and ASIC MoneySmart websites have helpful calculators to give you an idea of how much difference even a small amount can make to your retirement.

STEP 5: Take a look at what else you can do to boost your super. Do you have multiple super accounts? Does another fund offer the same investment mix with lower fees?

Chapter Summary

Super is a tax-effective way of saving for retirement. How much super you need depends on several factors, such as whether you are eligible for the age pension, whether you plan to fully retire or continue working part-time, and the age at which you want to retire. With medical advances, people are living longer and healthier lives, so one of your biggest risk factors is that you will outlive your super.

The best thing to do is put together a budget for yourself, imagining you are retired. Do you own your own home or are you renting? How much money would you like to set aside for things like travelling? Do you need to buy a new car or make any home improvements? Then, using these figures, you can have a play with a few online calculators to help you get an idea of how much you are likely to need in super in order to have an enjoyable retirement.

The sooner you start contributing to super, the better. Remember, the time the money has to grow is more important than how much you put in. Even a small amount can go a long way, but you need to start prioritising your super today.

Part Three:

Protecting Your Plans

CHAPTER SEVEN:

Safeguard Your Future

Now that you are on your way to building your dream life, let's take a look at the obstacles you may face along the way and now you can overcome them. In essence, it all comes down to protection, or insurance.

You have been conditioned to take out insurance for everything under the sun – including your house, your car, your possessions (home and contents) and your health. It's recommended that you take out travel insurance when you go on holiday, and many people also take out pet insurance to protect their pets. But what about protecting *you*?

When I talk to my clients, I'll often ask, 'What do you feel is your biggest asset? What is your most prized possession and something that you need to really protect?' Very rarely do I get the answer I'm looking for, which is: 'My ability to earn an income.' The ability to work is something that most people take for granted. But the reality is that many people find themselves unable to work because of accidents and illnesses, and all sorts of other things. This can have a serious impact on your family's financial wellbeing and can really put a dent in any plans you have for the future.

If you're not able to earn an income, how is that going to impact your life, your future, your wealth accumulation and your plans for your children? This is where insurance becomes invaluable. It's a core part of financial planning that many people tend to overlook, often because they find it too complicated or because they are worried that insurance companies won't pay the claim. The good news is that you can rest easy. According to ASIC, which conducted a review of the life insurance industry in 2016, ninety per cent of claims are paid in the first instance.

When it comes to insuring yourself, you have a few options. You can choose to self-insure, which means that you will use any investments or savings or money you've got access to to cover costs yourself if something happens. If you crash your car, if your house burns down, if you're sick and you can't go to work, you have decided that you have enough money to cover the costs yourself and don't need to pass on any of this risk to a third party (an insurance company).

Your second option is to pass on some of the risk, so having some savings in place and using insurance to top up any shortfall. For a premium, the insurance company has agreed to take on some of your risk. Your third option is to pass on all of the risk, whereby you take out full insurance cover and are insured to the eyeballs.

As a rule of thumb, you should insure anything you can't afford to replace. Most people tend to go with option two. The level of emergency savings you need will really depend on the level of insurance you are taking out.

In this chapter, I'll guide you through the four different types of insurance that you need to consider if you want to protect your family's financial future. They are income protection, critical illness insurance (also known as trauma cover), total and permanent disability insurance, and life insurance. I'll also run through how you can structure your insurances to make them more affordable, and what you can do to increase the chances of your claim being paid and how to expedite the process.

But, first, I want to share with you a personal lesson from my past.

My Biggest Mistake and the Lessons Learned

The biggest mistake I ever made was not paying enough attention to life insurance while I was young, fit and healthy. I first came across the term 'life insurance' when I was in my mid-twenties. I had just landed a corporate role at KPMG, and one of the perks was a life insurance policy and some income protection, paid for by the company. It was outlined in my letter of employment, yet I quickly forgot about it.

A couple of years into my tenure, I became quite ill. Eventually, I had to take extended time off work, which was a challenge in itself. Apart from the emotional challenge of not working, Simon and I were faced with a number of financial challenges. We were incurring significant medical bills that weren't covered by Medicare and only a small portion of which was covered by private health insurance.

Over the space of two years, I ended up taking over six months in unpaid leave, and once I returned to work I was only capable of doing so in a part-time capacity. It was only afterwards that I thought, 'Hang on. Didn't I have some sort of insurance in my super policy?' Yes, I did. But it was too late. My big mistake cost me a lot of heartache. But I did learn three valuable lessons as a result.

Lesson 1: Underwriting takes time

My first lesson was in the concept of underwriting, whereby an insurer conducts an assessment of your medical history to determine whether or not they will insure you. As my insurance was automatically put in place by my employer, I was never medically assessed by the insurance company. So it meant they had to do it once I lodged my claim. This process ended up taking nearly two years. Yes, you read that right.

First of all, there was a lot of paperwork. I had to fill in the specifics of my claim. My employer had to fill in specifics of my claim (they had to confirm my position, income, level of absenteeism and so on), and my doctor had to fill in details of my medical history. All this took time.

Underwriting is a key component of every form of life insurance. Do not be fooled by TV and online advertisements promoting how quick it is to get cover. Make no mistake: You will have to undergo extensive questioning regarding your medical history. The question is, would you rather spend time doing that now, when you don't urgently need a claim payment, or would you rather wait until you're sick and short of cash?

When you are looking at obtaining cover, be sure to find out when the medical assessment will take place and find an insurer that will conduct their investigations upfront.

Lesson 2: Pay attention to the fine print

The next lesson was in the importance of reading the fine print. One of the conditions of my income protection policy – which I wasn't aware of until later – was that I had to be off work for at least six months. Sadly, I kept trying to return to work, and in doing so I kept re-setting the clock on my waiting period. Also, my policy didn't cover me if I returned to work in a reduced capacity. The end result is that after a full two years, my insurance claim was finally paid, but it only reimbursed me for three weeks of lost income.

When it comes to income protection, you want to be familiar with things such as:

- The waiting period. This is how long you have to be off work before your claim starts, not to be confused with how long you have to wait before your claim is paid.

- The benefit period. This is how long your payment will be paid for. Let's say you are off work for five years. Will your income protection pay you for two years? Three years? Or however long you are off work?

- Will you be covered for loss of income?

- Do you have to use up your sick leave or can your claim be paid even while you are receiving other forms of income (such as sick leave pay or Centrelink support)?

Had I actually paid attention to my insurance policy, and taken appropriate steps and sought professional advice at the time, I could have received over $150,000 in compensation – instead of $3,000! How is this possible, you ask?

Lesson 3: Not all insurance policies are created equal

Because not all life insurance is the same.

Life insurance can be obtained from three different distribution channels, even if it is ultimately held with the same insurance company. The channel through which you obtain your cover will affect the cost, as well as the terms and conditions. These channels are known as direct (obtained directly from the insurer), group (obtained through your employer or super fund) and retail (obtained through a financial adviser).

I had a group policy, which meant it was subject to terms and conditions that my super fund had agreed to with the insurance company. Most super funds offer a default amount of cover, so you may not even realise that you already have some form of cover with your super, especially if you are with an industry super fund. The cover that you can get through super includes death cover (life insurance or term life), total and permanent disability cover, and income protection (also known as salary continuance).

In my case, this meant that while my cover in super had a long waiting period of six months and didn't compensate me for loss of income if I returned to work in a reduced capacity, there were other income protection policies that would have. This experience was a turning point for me, and was one of the reasons why I decided to become a financial adviser – to stop other women from making the same mistakes that I did! So, let's take a look at what you need to know in order to protect yourself financially.

The Ins and Outs of Life Insurance

There is no doubt that life insurance has to be the most complex and confusing insurance product out there. For starters, the term 'life Insurance' actually refers to four different types of life insurance! Basically, life insurance is there to protect you and your loved ones if things don't go according to plan. The four different policies you can choose from are:

- Life insurance (or death cover), whereby a lump sum is paid to your family when you die.

- Total and permanent disability (TPD) cover, whereby a lump sum is paid to you and your family if you are permanently disabled and can never work again.

- Income protection, whereby you are paid a regular income (in place of your salary) while you are off work for medical reasons.

- Trauma cover (sometimes called critical illness cover), whereby you are paid a lump sum if you are diagnosed with a serious condition like a heart condition or cancer.

Ultimately, you will probably need all four policies. With the exception of income protection, which is based on your income, it is completely up to you how much cover you take out. And, in all cases, you decide what the money is used for.

Maximising the benefits of insurance

The following case studies are designed to help you understand how you can use these insurance policies to your advantage.

John and Jane are a young married couple with two kids. They have a $300,000 mortgage and no other debts. John is the primary breadwinner and Jane is currently on unpaid maternity leave until the kids start school.

Scenario 1: What will happen to Jane and the kids if John dies tomorrow?

If John dies tomorrow, how will Jane support herself and the kids? John has $100,000 in super, which unfortunately isn't enough to pay off the mortgage. Jane can no longer afford to be a stay-at-home mum, but she can't even fathom the thought of finding a job and returning to work at such a sad and difficult time.

To avoid this situation, John and Jane could choose to take out life insurance for John. It must be sufficient to pay off the mortgage, and to provide Jane and the kids with enough money to support themselves for a particular length of time – whether it's six months or twenty years. John and Jane could also choose to take out life insurance for Jane. Again, it should be sufficient to pay off the mortgage and provide the family with enough income to cover living expenses, so that John can have some time off work to grieve and spend time with his children.

Here is an estimate of how much life insurance John needs:

Mortgage: $300,000

Twenty-four months of income for Jane: $300,000

Funeral costs: $20,000

Total costs to cover: $620,000, less John's superannuation payout of $100,000

Total life insurance required: $520,000

Scenario 2: What will happen if John has a stroke and can't return to work?

Under these circumstances, even if John is eligible for the disability pension, the maximum basic rate is approximately $800 a fortnight for singles and $600 a fortnight (each) for couples. Would you be able to pay your mortgage and bills – not to mention all your other expenses – on less than $400 a week? What would your life and your family's life look like if you were faced with that situation?

In addition to loss of income, John and Jane's home might require some modifications to make it wheelchair accessible (depending on the nature of John's disability). He may need in-home care, and he and Jane may need to buy a new car.

If John does not have an income protection policy that pays seventy-five per cent of his salary until he reaches retirement age, he and Jane should consider whether they'll need a lump-sum disability payment to help cover their ongoing living expenses for the foreseeable future, in addition to providing enough money to pay off the mortgage and afford John's care.

Here is an estimate of how much TPD insurance John needs:

Mortgage: $300,000

Twenty-four months of income for Jane (so she doesn't have to resume work straightaway): $300,000

Home modifications: $50,000

New car: $50,000

Total costs to cover: $700,000, less John's superannuation payout of $100,000

Total TPD insurance required: $600,000

Scenario 3: What will happen if John gets cancer and is off work for two years?

Assuming that John has a high survival rate, the costs that he and Jane might be faced with include out-of-pocket medical expenses (not all treatments are covered by Medicare or private hospital cover), the cost of travel and accommodation to see specialists who may be located interstate or even overseas, daily living expenses, and personal loan or mortgage repayments.

The reality is that, even with Medicare in place, most people still have significant out-of-pocket expenses when it comes to healthcare. Also, it often takes a while before medicines become available through the Pharmaceutical Benefits Scheme, or PBS, and through Medicare. There are also extensive waiting lists to get treatments. And even if you are fully covered by Medicare and private hospital cover, this doesn't cover your loss of income. That's why it's so important to have the necessary insurance in place.

To reduce the stress on John and Jane, they could take out income protection insurance for John (covering seventy-five per cent of his income) and sufficient trauma insurance to cover the estimated cost of treatment.

The calculations for John's trauma cover might look something like this:

Two years of income protection top-up (salary x 25% x 2) = $75,000
Estimated cost of treatment and travel: $150,000
Total trauma cover: $225,000

Depending on the cost of the trauma cover, John and Jane could also choose to pay off the mortgage at this time as well, in which case they would take out $555,000 in cover. John can also choose to add up to $150,000 cover for each child over the age of one. If John doesn't have an income protection policy, then he could choose to take out even higher trauma cover, to provide him with enough income to cover all living expenses while he is off work.

According to AMP, in 2017 the average trauma claim payment was $181,892, so this may be a useful guide as to how much is reasonable.

Scenario 4: What will happen if John suffers from clinical depression and is off work for eighteen months?

Mental health is among the leading causes of income protection claims. In this case, John wouldn't qualify for a life or trauma payout, and whether or not he can access TPD cover will depend on the severity and duration of his depression. Income protection is the main form of cover to protect John's income in this case.

Scenario 5: What will happen to John and the kids if Jane is diagnosed with cancer?

A common belief among women is that only the main breadwinner needs to be insured. However, this cannot be further from the truth. While Jane may not give herself sufficient credit for the hard work she does, the fact is that stay-at-home parents *do* make a significant contribution to the household (and the economy at large). A recent PricewaterhouseCoopers report found that women perform three quarters of all unpaid work, and put the value of unpaid childcare alone at $345 billion.

If Jane is sick and unable to look after the kids, the family would find themselves not only in need of someone to help look after Jane, but also help look after the kids and the household while John is at work. Even if John has income protection, his policy will not cover him if he takes time off work to look after Jane and the kids. Either way, the family is likely to find themselves facing out-of-pocket medical expenses, as well as the need to supplement John's income and pay for the cost of childcare.

As a stay-at-home parent, Jane is not eligible for income protection. However, she is able to take out life insurance, total and permanent disability insurance, and trauma cover.

The calculations for Jane's insurance might look something like this:

Trauma cover

Estimated cost of medical treatment: $150,000

Cost of two years of full-time childcare for two kids: $104,000

Six months of income replacement for John: $75,000

Total trauma cover required: $329,000

Life insurance cover

Mortgage: $300,000

Twenty-four months of income for John: $300,000

Funeral costs: $20,000

Total costs to cover: $620,000, less Jane's superannuation payout of $30,000

Total life insurance required: $590,000

Total and permanent disability cover

Mortgage: $300,000

Twenty-four months of income for John (so he doesn't have to resume work straightaway): $300,000

Home modifications: $50,000

New car: $50,000

Total costs to cover: $700,000, less Jane's superannuation payout of $30,000

Total TPD insurance required: $670,000

Regardless of which forms of cover you opt for, you want to make sure that you fully understand what you are and are not covered for, and really read that fine print. Keep in mind that even if you are covered by your work, that cover will cease when you change employers.

> **BONUS RESOURCE:** To help you understand your insurance needs better, download your free insurance calculator at womenwithcents. com.au/wonderwoman. This will help you to determine whether the insurance you have in place is likely to be sufficient to meet your needs.

Making Insurance More Affordable

When I look at the finances of middle- and low-income families, I hear a lot of this: 'I can't afford $2,000 a year in premiums.' And yet I see those same families spending money on other, arguably unnecessary, items. The mum with multiple prams. The couple with gym and Foxtel memberships. It goes on.

It would seem to me, then, that it's not an issue of affordability, but the fact that we value other things over insurance. In other words, we place more value on the things that will satisfy us right now, rather than putting money aside for something that may or may not happen in the future. But the way I see it, you can't afford *not* to have insurance.

CASE STUDY: SARAH'S STORY

I'm a married mum of three. At the time of my accident, I was thirty-six years old and working as a paraplanner. My kids were aged four weeks, three and seven at the time.

Getting T-boned on my way home from the post office was the last thing I expected to happen, yet there I was. Initially I was in shock and thought I was okay, and so I went home. Within five minutes, the pain in my head and neck began. Upon seeing a doctor, I was told I had whiplash. A few weeks later, the pain in my head had worsened, and I had pins and needles in both arms and hands.

My ability to work was gone. I couldn't concentrate, nor could I sit at my desk for hours and hours like I was used to doing. I also couldn't lift my three-year-old or do menial tasks around the house. Even grocery shopping was a challenge, as I couldn't push the trolley or lift heavy bags. One night, as I was lying awake due to the relentless stabbing pain, I thought to myself, 'I wonder if my income protection would cover this?'

I called my insurer and explained what had happened. They made the process so easy and gave me a case worker to work with. Not only was my claim processed quickly, the insurer has been instrumental in my recovery, which has taken three years – longer than expected due to reactions to the medication and other setbacks. The insurer has provided further assistance in the form of exercise physiologists and occupational therapists.

Having income protection and the ongoing help from my insurer has allowed me to continue to provide for my family of five. Without it, I can't imagine where we'd be.

According to the Australian Institute of Health and Welfare, chronic diseases are the leading cause of ill health, disability and death, affecting more than fifty per cent of the population and affecting women more than men (fifty-two per cent compared to forty-eight per cent). Meanwhile, one in three Australians are disabled for more than three months during their working life. It's important to note that disabilities and illnesses aren't just physical. In addition to things like cancer and musculoskeletal conditions, depression or anxiety could force you to take time off work.

Again, I want you to stop and think about this very seriously, and imagine how your family would cope financially if something happened to you. You may be off work for much longer than three months – it could be years or even permanently. What is that going to mean for you and your family's financial situation? What is your life going to look like?

With that in mind, there are things you can do to make insurance more affordable and get more bang for your buck. Let's take a look.

Choose the right channel from the outset

When deciding where to buy your life insurance from, it is important to distinguish between cost and value. As I mentioned earlier, there are three channels you can buy life insurance through. Group policies obtained through super tend to be low cost. However, this is because they come with more fine print and fewer features. For example, an income protection policy may require you to be off work for an extended period of time and may only pay your claim for two years, which could be problematic if you are off work for longer than that.

In a similar fashion to group policies, direct policies – which you apply for online or on the phone with the insurance company – may appear to be a quick solution, but again they often come with limitations. Also, direct policies tend to be more expensive because it costs the insurance company a lot more to get your business. Direct policies are typically advertised on TV, radio and the Internet. However, these advertisements cost a lot of money, so these costs are then passed on to you, the consumer.

In my experience, retail policies tend to be the best option. The retail product – which you can only access through a financial adviser or insurance broker – will offer you better value for money, more comprehensive cover, less fine print and lower premiums. You will also get an upfront assessment, which means that insurance companies will process your application in a lot more detail. As a result, you will know exactly what you are and are not covered for.

Financial advisers also have a direct relationship with the underwriters and claim assessors at the insurance companies, which can be a huge help as far as having someone to represent your case and help push your application and claim through.

While financial advisers do get paid a commission, the same way mortgage brokers get paid a commission from the bank, this is nothing to be concerned about. Retail products will always come with a commission component, regardless of whether you're seeing a financial adviser face to face or comparing products on an online comparison site. The way I see it, this commission is there to ensure you receive sound financial advice and to get support at claim time.

My personal preference has always been to have a strong, ongoing relationship with an adviser, who will be there to look after me year on year and help out at claim time as well.

HOT TIP: Once you have insurance in place, I would caution against switching insurance providers too often. This is because life insurance does not cover you for pre-existing conditions. By changing providers every few years, you run the risk of no longer being covered. So, my advice is to play it safe and stay put. If you do decide to change providers, make sure that your new policy is fully medically assessed, and do not cancel your existing policy until you have written confirmation that your new policy is in force.

Structure your insurance correctly

How you structure your insurance can have a huge impact on the cost. This is where it's important to understand the difference between stepped premiums and level premiums. Basically, a stepped premium will go up over the years as you age (and the chances of you making a claim increase), meaning it is cheaper in the short term. With a level premium, the premium is locked in (to a large extent) based on your age at the time you take out cover. This means that it can be more expensive than a stepped premium in the short term.

However, if you plan on holding your cover until you retire, then level premiums can be significantly cheaper. While your premiums will still go up slightly each year (due to inflation, if the insurance company changes premiums for your age bracket or if you get a pay rise), it's not going to go up as much as a stepped premium.

With a level premium, if you are taking out insurance as a thirty-five-year-old female, you will, for the life of that policy, pay premiums at the level of a thirty-five-year-old. So, when you're forty, you will still be charged at the level of a thirty-five-year-old female.

So, from a cost-saving perspective, which type of premium structure should you opt for? Basically, stepped is cheaper in the short term, but far more expensive in the long term (often by tens of thousands of dollars). Level is cheaper in the long term, but more expensive in the short term (often by several hundred dollars or more per year).

If you choose a level premium, keep in mind that for about five to ten years, you will be paying a higher premium than you would be if you were on a stepped premium. But over the long term, it will be the cheaper option for you.

Remember, financial planning is all about strategy. Not having a short-term view, but really looking at the long term and mapping out your strategy accordingly. That could not be truer than when it comes to looking at how you structure your life insurances and whether you take out a stepped or a level premium.

Consider your payment options

Often, you can receive additional discounts for paying your insurance policies annually rather than monthly, as well as bundling multiple policies with the same provider. Also, if you hold a retail policy, you have the choice of paying the premiums from your super. There are two main reasons why you would consider paying for your insurance policies through super:

- **Maximise tax deductions**. With the exception of income protection, life insurance policies are not tax-deductible for individuals. However, super funds are able to claim a tax deduction for life, TPD and income protection policies (trauma cover is not available through super). For this reason, it can be advantageous to pay for these policies through your super fund and, in doing so, access a fifteen per cent tax deduction on those policies (which essentially means a fifteen per cent discount on your premiums).

- **Ease cash flow**. It is also easier on your cash flow, which is particularly handy if you're starting a family, on extended maternity leave, down to a single income or in any other situation where cash flow is tight. Having insurance that is funded through super can be an effective way of insuring yourself without affecting your cash flow, because you don't have to pay the premiums out of your take-home pay. But, on the flipside, this means that the premiums are basically reducing your super balance. In this case, you should look at making extra contributions into your super fund to cover those premiums in the long term. Otherwise, they will eat away at your retirement funds. (Be careful, however, that you do not exceed the super contribution caps, as discussed in chapter six.)

HOT TIP: If you are a high-income earner and likely to exceed the contribution cap, you may be better off holding your income protection policy outside of super and claiming a tax deduction on your income tax return instead.

ACTION ITEM: CONTACT YOUR SUPER FUND AND CHECK YOUR INSURANCE

STEP 1: Sit down and consider what the financial impact would be on you and your family if the unexpected happened. Consider how much time off work you would like to have and what expenses you would need to cover. Write these down under each category of life, TPD and trauma and then add them up.

STEP 2: Call your super fund and check how much life, TPD and income protection insurance you have. What are the terms of your income protection? How long do you have to be off work? And what are the waiting and benefit periods?

STEP 3: If you haven't already, inform your super fund of your occupation. Otherwise, you are likely to be paying higher premiums, as you will be placed in a high-risk category by default.

STEP 4: Review and update your insurance. Is the cover you have sufficient to meet your needs? If not, book an appointment with a financial adviser and conduct a full review of your insurances.

Chapter Summary

Life insurance is a tricky area to navigate. It can be difficult to know whether you are comparing apples with apples because there is so much fine print involved. This is one area that I strongly recommend you seek professional advice on, rather than doing it yourself. Getting professional advice will give you a far better understanding of the differences between policies, and ensure you get value for money as well as support when you need to make a claim.

Before taking out an insurance policy, give thought to how much cover you are likely to need as well as how much cover you can realistically afford. Quite often, it is about striking a balance between your current and your future cash flow needs. Keep in mind that the less cover you decide to take out, the more you will need in emergency savings.

CHAPTER EIGHT:

Estate Planning

Did you know that Australia is on the brink of the largest intergenerational wealth transfer in its history? *The Australian Financial Review* recently reported that an estimated *$3 trillion* is due to change hands over the next ten to twenty years, with women expected to be the main recipients, simply due to the fact that we typically live longer than men.

This is why there has never been a more important time for women to take notice of financial matters, including estate planning. It is important not just from the point of view of putting together your own will and estate plan, but also to help your family members implement theirs. After all, there is a strong possibility that, at some stage in your life, you will stand to receive an inheritance or be required to assist with distributing a family member's estate.

Knowing what the options are and what questions to ask is critical to enabling you not only to ease your family's stress at a very sad and difficult time, but also make sure the inheritance is managed in the most effective manner.

No one likes to contemplate their own mortality. However, try to think of estate planning in another way. As women, we are natural nurturers and would do anything to protect our loved ones. This is one more way we can do that – by taking care of the unpleasant stuff now, so our loved ones won't have to. As the saying goes, there are only two guarantees in life – death and taxes. That's what the topic of estate planning is all about (this is a great time to pause and grab yourself a glass of wine!).

Estate planning involves more than just writing a will. Estate planning is the planning and documenting of a strategy to ensure that, when you die, the right assets pass to the right people at the right time. This means that you need to consider the beneficiaries' personal circumstances, as well as the impact of debt and tax in the context of fairness. Allow me to explain what I mean by this, using a hypothetical example.

A mother wants her son and daughter to inherit an equal portion of her estate. She decides to leave $300,000 in super to her adult son, and her home – which is also worth $300,000 – to her daughter. While this may seem fair, the tax implications for each form of inheritance are different. If the daughter sells the home tax free, she gets $300,000 clean and clear. But the son is liable to pay tax of around $50,000 on his inheritance. Is that fair? No. This is why estate planning is so important, as it can address these sorts of discrepancies and prevent family arguments from erupting.

As women, we are natural nurturers and would do anything to protect our loved ones. This is one more way we can do that – by taking care of the unpleasant stuff, so our loved ones don't have to.

You also need to consider whether the beneficiaries are in a position to accept the inheritance. For example, they may be going through a divorce, facing bankruptcy, or struggling with an addiction or gambling problem.

Let's say a parent wants to leave money to their adult daughter, who is in the middle of a divorce. Do they want to leave money to the daughter's spouse? Of course not. Or let's say a parent wants to leave money to their son, who runs a business and is at risk of bankruptcy. Do they want the money going to creditors? No. Or perhaps the beneficiary is simply too young (in which case the money could be held in trust until they reach a particular age). Take, for example, a parent with a twenty-year-old child. Is a twenty-year-old mature enough to handle an inheritance or are they likely to spend the money unwisely?

These are the sorts of situations that, as part of estate planning, you need to take into consideration ahead of time. This is why it's important to put a strategy in place – to ensure your wishes are carried out in the way you intended. In this chapter, I'll explain why you need a will, how to make a valid will and update it, and some of the most common mistakes made in relation to will kits, as well as your options for minimising tax on an inheritance. But, first, let's discuss what needs to happen when someone dies.

The Logistics of Death

Let's begin by having a chat about what needs to happen when someone dies, because there are a few administrative things that need to take place. If the deceased was receiving a pension or disability support, the relevant government agencies need to be notified. The death certificate will need to be issued. The relevant banks need to be notified. If the deceased had any bank accounts held solely in their name, those accounts will be frozen. However, banks are usually willing to release any funds needed to pay for funeral costs, if that's what is needed.

> **HOT TIP:** If your savings or pay cheques are sitting in a bank account that is only in your partner's name, those accounts are likely to be frozen upon their death, leaving you without access to cash in the short term. To avoid this situation, make sure you have money going into a jointly held account or some savings in your own name.

181

The funeral will need to be arranged, and the will needs to be found and probate applied for so that the estate can begin to be distributed.

From the outset, this part can be challenging for families as most people often don't discuss their finances or their wishes with their loved ones. This is especially true when someone dies unexpectedly – family members find themselves faced with making important decisions around medical care, organ donation and funeral arrangements without knowing the person's true wishes.

Knowing what income the person was receiving, what assets and bank accounts they had, and who needs to be notified of their passing can also be a challenging task if the information is hard to find. This is why it is so important for families to be informed and to discuss their circumstances and wishes with each other.

Why You Need a Will

You need a will so that you can have control over how your assets will be distributed when you die. It enables you to appoint guardians for minor children, rather than leaving it to the courts to decide. You can choose whom to entrust with the role of executor (the person responsible for carrying out the instructions of the will). And they can expedite the grant of probate.

Probate is a document issued to the executor by the relevant supreme court, giving the executor authority to take control of the deceased person's estate and distribute the assets in accordance with the terms of the will. Before anything can be done, the executor will go to the courts to apply for probate and then they can proceed with administering the estate. Without a will, obtaining probate can sometimes drag on for months.

Furthermore, if you die without a will (known as dying intestate), the law in each state sets out how your estate will be distributed after all debts are paid, which could result in your assets being distributed to unintended beneficiaries.

In New South Wales, for example, if you only have a spouse and no children, your spouse will inherit the entire estate. If you have a spouse and children, your spouse will still inherit the entire estate. If you have a spouse and children from another relationship, then up to $350 000, plus personal effects and half of the balance of the estate, will go to your spouse. The children will receive the remaining fifty per cent equally.

If you don't have a spouse, then the order of distribution is:

1. Children
2. Parents
3. Brothers and sisters
4. Grandparents
5. Uncles and aunts
6. First cousins

CASE STUDY: SUSAN'S STORY

I'm fifty years old and a widowed mum of two young girls. I was forty-four years old when my husband was diagnosed with motor neurone disease, for which there is no cure. At the time, I was working as a public servant and my husband owned a smash repair business. We had a mortgage on our house and a mortgage on the business.

We both stopped working and dissolved the business upon learning of his diagnosis. I cannot put into words how devastating a diagnosis of MND is. It is a particularly cruel disease, which causes progressive muscle wasting. Sufferers live on average for two to three years following their diagnosis, and are typically completely paralysed at the end of their life. This means it takes the sufferer's ability to walk, talk and ultimately breathe. My husband's progression followed this typical path, and he passed away two and a half years after he was diagnosed.

Having to contemplate such a horrific way to die is unfathomable. Having to describe this in a way that our children could understand is something I would never wish upon anyone. Fortunately, we at least had comprehensive insurance and started receiving payments from our insurer almost immediately after Scott's diagnosis. Our policy included trauma cover, income protection and life insurance. This took the pressure off us financially and enabled us to get the best care possible for Scott, as well as spend invaluable time together as a family.

Both Scott and I had/have a will. Upon Scott's diagnosis, we double checked that this was all in order – and made sure that it included guardians of our children, should something happen to me as well. All of this is awfully confronting. I could not believe at the time that it was happening, and still sometimes wake up and can't believe it (and it's been over three years since Scott passed away). However, because all of Scott's wishes were documented in his will, it made the execution of it – upon his passing – very straightforward. I continued to have access to our family's finances without any interruption.

Making a Valid Will

As you can see, it is extremely important to have a valid will in place. Let's talk about how you can do that.

First of all, your will has to be in writing and it has to be signed by you in the presence of two witnesses who cannot be beneficiaries. This is a very important part of the process, yet many people get it wrong, especially when they do wills on their own without the assistance of a lawyer. They often get beneficiaries (those who stand to receive the inheritance) to witness their will and this makes the will invalid. Make sure that the will is signed in the presence of two witnesses who are *not* beneficiaries. You also need to make sure that all three of you have witnessed each other's signatures.

There are a number of things to consider when writing your will. This includes whom you will appoint as executor. The executor needs to be at least eighteen years old and be of sound mind. When you're considering whom to appoint as an executor, it's always wise to choose someone who is likely to outlive you and someone who lives in your state, as that will make it easier for them to administer the estate. Ideally, you should appoint someone who you believe has enough knowledge and financial literacy to be able to administer the estate.

Executor duties typically include looking after funeral arrangements and obtaining probate. This will involve a few documents, including the summons applying for probate, the death certificate, the original will, the statement of assets and liabilities of the deceased, and the affidavit by the executor concerning the will.

The executor will need to identify and collect the deceased's assets, and take possession of and store any valuables (like jewellery). They will also need to contact the relevant financial institutions to notify them of the person's death. They will need to settle debts in accordance with the relevant rules, and, if applicable, notify government agencies such as Centrelink. They also need to prepare tax returns and pay all taxes. They will be responsible for distributing assets to beneficiaries – so this includes any cash legacies, distributions to testamentary trusts and distributions to residuary heirs.

For this reason, it is very important and useful to keep a record of all your bank accounts, your insurances, and contact details for your lawyer, accountant and financial planner. You should also store the will in a safe place, which your family knows about – there is no point in having a will if nobody knows it exists or can find it. It's a good idea to give a copy of the will to the beneficiaries to make things a bit smoother.

Consider who you would like to be guardians for any minor children. As a parent, I understand this is a very, very difficult topic for many people, and it's the reason why many people put off writing a will altogether. Perhaps it makes you too uncomfortable, or you can't decide who would be best to appoint as guardians. Perhaps you don't want to upset any family members or put anyone in an uncomfortable situation, so you end up putting it off entirely.

Nevertheless, resist the urge to bury your head in the sand. It is a very, very important aspect of your will, and you want to have as much say as possible. As hard as it is, I strongly encourage you to rip off the Band-Aid, sit down and have those conversations, and get it sorted. You will sleep much better after it's done.

The following real-life example highlights why it's so important to nominate guardians for minor children. In January 2004, a family's four-wheel drive overturned on the Hume Highway in New South Wales, killing both parents and two of their four children. The surviving daughters were aged thirteen and seven. Thankfully, the parents had a will and had appointed guardians for their children in the event of their death. Without a will, in the midst of this tragedy, the surviving daughters and their extended family would have been put through guardianship hearings in the ACT Civil and Administrative Tribunal.

HOT TIP: When you prepare your will, it is a good idea to also put in place an Enduring Power of Attorney and Enduring Power of Guardianship (also known as Medical Power of Attorney). These documents will enable someone you trust to make financial and medical decisions on your behalf in case you are unable to do so yourself (for example, due to being in a coma or suffering dementia). Before appointing this person, make sure you speak with them about your wishes so that they are better able act on your behalf.

Also, consider which assets are going to form part of your estate, and whether you should pass these assets on or retain them within a trust. For example, testamentary trusts can provide a greater level of control over the distribution of assets to beneficiaries. This is where legal and financial advice can really help you decide whether it is necessary or a good idea.

TESTAMENTARY TRUSTS

While a testamentary trust is established under a will, it does not come into effect until after the death of the person making the will. A testamentary trust can offer beneficiaries greater flexibility and control as to when and how they take their inheritance. It can offer protection from will changes, and protect assets in the event of beneficiary divorce, creditor protection and so on. There are also tax advantages to having a testamentary trust.

However, there are a couple of things to keep in mind. A testamentary trust can be expensive to administer. The trustee has control of the trust, so they should be someone who will act in the best interest of the beneficiaries. It is very important to get legal and tax advice, and also see your financial adviser, to determine whether a testamentary trust is appropriate for your circumstances.

Give thought to whether some beneficiaries have special needs. As I touched on earlier, you may have family members who are too young to inherit the estate, are ill, are going through divorce or bankruptcy, or have gambling or addiction issues. These are all things to give thought to and plan for. Again, this is where a lawyer can really help you.

Finally, give thought to whether it is likely or possible that anyone is going to challenge the estate (such as a former spouse or children from a previous relationship). If you suspect someone may, make sure you have a chat to your lawyer to ensure you're protecting your wishes as best as possible.

Should You Use a Will Kit?

Will kits allow you to prepare your own will and are often sold at post offices, news agencies and online for about thirty dollars, making them a cheap and seemingly more convenient option. However, it can be risky to use will kits or prepare a will yourself using another method, such as online templates.

When it comes to the death of a family member, a sad reality is that arguments over money can often erupt and this can lead to someone contesting the will. Using a will kit can make it easier to challenge the estate by bringing into question the validity of the will. DIY wills can often be ambiguous, incorrectly completed or witnessed, and can make it easier to raise questions of whether the will maker had the adequate capacity to prepare the will or was under any undue influence or duress.

Let's go through some of the most common mistakes people make.

For starters, will kits are often incorrectly signed and witnessed. As I mentioned before, the common mistake people make is getting a beneficiary to witness their signature on their will. This automatically makes the will invalid.

Often, there is a failure to appoint an executor, or people make the mistake of appointing the wrong type of person. For example, they appoint someone who lives on the other side of the country, or someone underage. People also make the mistake of giving away jointly owned assets, such as property, which you can't give away as part of your will. Also, because the templates provided by will kits tend to be very basic, they don't cater for blended families, for minors, for family trusts, for any assets that are held by a business, superannuation, life insurance – the list goes on.

They also omit the residuary clause, which addresses anything that has been omitted or left out in the portioning of the estate (in other words, you haven't addressed who will inherit it). If any part of the estate is remaining, the residuary clause addresses who is going to receive it.

Unfortunately, as well as taking up a lot of time, challenges to the estate can cost thousands in legal fees, which may have to be paid for from the estate. For this reason, I suggest getting legal and financial advice when putting together an estate plan, in order to make sure that the will is properly documented and that potentials for family disputes are identified upfront and mitigated as much as possible. Doing this will save everyone a great deal of stress (and money) in the long run.

ACTION ITEM: GET YOUR AFFAIRS IN ORDER

STEP 1: Make sure that you have an 'important documents' checklist. Put together a list with all of your important details, so that your family knows who your accountant is, who your financial adviser is, who your lawyer is, where your will can be found, what bank accounts you have, what assets you have and so on. This will make the process much easier for your family.

BONUS RESOURCE: Download an 'important documents' checklist at womenwithcents.com.au/wonderwoman.

STEP 2: If there are assets such as shares or property that someone will stand to inherit, detail where they can find all the necessary information about those assets. Again, this will make it much easier for them to process tax returns and other administrative tasks.

STEP 3: Have a chat to your family about your wishes, including organ donation and funeral plans. By doing this now, it'll be one less thing for your family to worry about later.

STEP 4: Review and, if necessary, update your binding and non-binding nominations in your super fund. Make a note n your diary to update your binding nominations in writing every three years.

STEP 5: Have a chat to your family members about their situations as well. If they have a will and other important documents, find out where they can be found.

STEP 6: Book an appointment with a lawyer to prepare (or update) your will. Make a note in your calendar each year to check whether your will requires any changes, in case your circumstances nave changed.

Tax Considerations

I mentioned before that estate planning requires you to consider the impact of tax on fairness, so let's briefly run through how an inheritance is taxed.

But, first, let me be clear that this section of the book is intended as a guide only. Tax is an extremely complex area, so please make sure you get financial and tax advice regarding your particular circumstances, because any number of variables and nuances can change how the tax laws apply.

When it comes to tax on an inheritance, it will depend on whether it's an inheritance from super or assets outside of super.

An Inheritance from Super

If the inheritance is from super, it will be tax-free if paid to a dependent under tax law. This is not to be confused with the definition of a dependent as applicable under the superannuation laws (in other words, super will only be paid to a dependent).

In this case, we are talking under tax law. An inheritance from super will be tax-free if paid to a dependent as deemed under the tax law. This can be your spouse, children under the age of eighteen, children over eighteen who can prove they were financially dependent on you, and anyone else over eighteen who can prove they were financially dependent on you or interdependent. If the inheritance is from super and is paid to a non-dependent, then things get a little bit more complicated.

If you take a look at your super statement, you will notice that your super is split into two main components, called the tax-free component and the taxable component. This means that how the super was taxed previously will affect how much tax is payable when the super is paid out.

The tax-free component is obviously tax-free, whereas the taxable component will be taxed at either fifteen per cent or thirty per cent, plus the Medicare levy, and this will depend on whether the super fund has already taxed or paid tax on that money.

HOT TIP: Pre-retirees can commence what's called a redistribution strategy into super, which allows them to increase the tax-free component in their super. This strategy involves taking money out of super and then putting it back in, so it's re-classed as a tax-free component. This means that adult kids will then inherit more money tax-free. This is an area where it's really important to seek financial advice and get help to put the strategy in place. If you're talking to your parents about their estate planning, get them to have a look at this area so that, if you're an adult child of theirs who isn't financially dependent, you're inheriting as much of that super as possible tax-free.

Assets Outside Super

If inheriting assets outside of super, different tax rules will apply depending on the nature of the asset and when it was originally acquired. In the case of cash, any cash that you have inherited wi.. be tax-free. In the case of property or shares, there will be capital gains tax payable when you sell that property or those shares. If you inherit a principal residence, then it is generally tax-free if you sell it within two years of inheriting it. Otherwise, capital gains tax may apply, depending on whether you lived in it or own any other properties.

I would like to take this opportunity to clarify that capital gains tax is not a separate tax, as many people tend to think, given the way the phrase is used. Basically, what happens when you sell an asset is that the capital gain or, in other words, the profit that you make is added to your taxable income and then you pay tax on your total assessable income at your marginal rate. That's how capital gains tax works. It is not a separate tax to income tax that you need to go and pay.

How you calculate the capital gain depends on when that asset was bought. Was it bought before 1985, before capital gains tax was introduced, or was it bought after 1985? If the asset you inherited was bought before 1985, then the gross capital gain is the sale price less the market value on the date of death. If the inherited asset was bought after 1985, then the gross capital gain is the sale price less the original purchase price, and a fifty per cent discount applies if the asset was purchased more than a year ago.

Again, just to re-emphasise, capital gain is a complex area with too many ins and outs to explain in this section, so make sure you speak to your tax accountant for specific advice.

Investment Bonds

Investment bonds are often used by high-income earners who have a long-term investment timeframe (over ten years). They are very popular with parents and grandparents when it comes to saving money for children's education.

I have included them in this chapter because, in addition to being a tax-effective investment vehicle for high-income earners, they can also be a particularly useful tool for estate planning. They can offer tax advantages, as well as simplicity and cost-effectiveness compared to holding assets in your own name that later form part of your estate. While investment bonds have many uses, from an estate planning perspective, they can be particularly useful for blended families or grandparents wanting to invest some money for their grandchildren.

An investment bond (often called an insurance bond) is basically a managed fund, which is linked to a life insurance policy. The investment bond (not to be confused with government or corporate bonds) is subject to specific tax rules. Much like your super, an investment bond is its own entity that sits outside of your estate, meaning you don't have to declare that investment on your tax return and it doesn't get tied up in the event that you die intestate or the will is challenged.

The bond will pay tax at thirty per cent on your investment earnings within the fund. They are easy to establish, and you can start off with a small initial investment, usually around $1,000 (although this can vary among investment bond providers). You also have a choice of investment options, just as you do with a standard managed fund. If you hold it for ten years or more, after the ten-year mark, you can withdraw that money tax-free without having to pay any further tax. However, special tax rules apply if you withdraw the money before the ten-year period is up.

If you withdraw before eight years, it means that any investment gain will be taxed at your marginal tax rate. This is the tax rate you pay as an individual based on your income and which tax bracket you fall into. You will be taxed at your specific tax rate, but you will receive a thirty per cent offset, so you're not doubling up on tax. If you withdraw in the ninth year, then two thirds of the gain is taxable and you will receive a thirty per cent offset. If you withdraw in the tenth year, it means one third of the gain is taxable. If you withdraw after ten years, then that money is withdrawn fully tax-free, so you're getting any profits tax-free.

However, investment bonds come with a specific rule around how much you can contribute. You can only contribute 125 per cent of what you put in the previous year. If you break that rule, and in one year you decide to invest more than 125 per cent of the previous year's contribution, you will restart that ten-year period.

It also means that, if one year you stop contributing altogether, then you can't contribute anymore. Let's say you have been contributing regularly for five years and then in year six you didn't put anything in. You now have two choices. You either have to resume that ten-year investment timeframe or you would have to start a new investment bond and leave the money that you've invested there so far and then wait another three years and withdraw it tax-free.

Now that you have an understanding of what investment bonds are about, let's take a look at some of their estate planning advantages. For starters, your investment is linked to a life insurance policy, so your nominated beneficiary will receive the proceeds from that investment tax-free. Also, it sits separately from your estate, meaning that it's protected from creditors in the event of bankruptcy. And upon your death, the funds will be paid directly to your nominated beneficiary, and will not be affected by intestacy laws or someone challenging your will.

Binding and Non-binding Nominations

As mentioned previously, your super sits outside of your estate and is not distributed according to your will. The trustee of the super fund will pay the death benefit (super paid after a person's death) according to the fund rules, which determine who the money can go to and the order of priority.

The binding death benefit nomination is the only way to override trustee discretion. If you haven't made a valid binding death benefit nomination before you die, then it's up to the trustee of your super fund to determine whom the money will go to. You can also make a non-binding death benefit nomination. This is basically a suggestion or a guide, but, ultimately, the trustee decides whom the money should be paid to.

If the nomination is valid, the trustee has to follow it, even if your circumstances have changed. This is why it's very important to stay on top of your finances and update your paperwork if your situation changes at any point. I will give you a particular example. Let's say you've made a binding death benefit nomination for the money to go to your spouse, but then you separate. While your intentions may have changed, if you die before obtaining a divorce, that nomination is binding unless it has been amended, has been revoked or has expired.

That's one example where you can be caught out. So, it is very important to make sure that, if your situation has changed, you update all of the necessary paperwork. Otherwise, you may find that the death benefit goes to someone you no longer wish for it to go to.

In order to make a valid binding death benefit nomination, it's not enough to just fill out the relevant form. It has to be valid and, in order to be valid, it has to satisfy certain criteria. First of all, you can only nominate a dependent or your estate. A dependent, under Australian superannuation laws, could be your spouse or a child (including adult children). Someone who may be financially dependent on you can also be a dependent.

You have to renew it every three years. If you're going through your paperwork now, and filling everything out, maybe put a reminder in your calendar three years from now, so you don't forget to update it. I actually recommend putting in place a reminder for yourself every year, just to do a bit of a sanity check on your finances and check whether anything has changed. For example, have you got a new spouse? Have you separated? Has anything happened that would warrant an update to your binding death benefit nomination or any other relevant paperwork?

Finally, the nomination has to be in writing – you can't just leave a voicemail for the relevant super fund and say what you want to have done. It has to be signed by you, in the presence of two adult witnesses who are not beneficiaries. If you're filling it out and you're nominating your spouse, they can't witness the nomination. Otherwise, it's not binding.

It also has to be sent to the trustee. If you have filled it out, it's been witnessed properly and it's in writing, but it hasn't been sent to the trustee yet, there is no binding death benefit nomination in place if you die. That's a very important thing to remember. It's not enough to just fill it out and have it sitting in a filing cabinet. You have to send it off to the trustee.

Updating Your Will

Another estate planning myth is that once the will is drawn up, you can forget about it. On the contrary, your will is certainly not a case of set and forget. Really, you want to review your will at least every two to three years to make sure that it is still appropriate for your needs.

You also want to update your will every time your circumstances change. This includes a marriage, separation or divorce, starting a new de facto relationship, having children or grandchildren, or the death of a spouse. Or perhaps the executor you have appointed is no longer able to carry out the responsibility – either they've died or become ill. Or perhaps someone you've intended to inherit your estate has passed away, so you need to amend your will to cater for that. Also, your children may have married or got divorced.

There are a couple of things to keep in mind with regard to marriage and divorce:

- A marriage separation does not affect your will, even though your intentions may have changed. This is something that many people are not even aware of. Keep in mind that if you do have a will in place and you have separated from your spouse, it may be time to go and update your will.

- Marriage will revoke a will unless the will was made in anticipation of marriage. Again, many people have a will, but they had it done when they were single. Then they get married and forget that, in that case, the act of the marriage has actually revoked the will (unless you actually write something in your will along the lines of 'I am making this will in anticipation of…'). If you haven't made it clear that you have written that will in anticipation of your upcoming or future marriage, then marriage will revoke that will.

- Divorce will only cancel gifts to a former spouse or, if you have appointed your now ex-spouse as an executor, divorce will only affect those aspects of your will. It will not revoke your will.

There's also a list of things you need to do in order to prepare for your own death. I understand this is a very difficult topic to think about and discuss.

None of us like to think or talk about these sorts of things, particularly with our family. Unfortunately, it is a necessary part of life. For that reason, it is very important to take the time now to ensure your financial affairs are in order, and have the necessary conversations with your family.

Chapter Summary

As you can see, there are a number of factors to be considered when putting together a will and an estate plan. This is why it is so important not to put together a will by yourself, but to really seek out financial and legal advice, and to be strategic with this, as with every other aspect of financial planning.

Sit down, have a look at your circumstances and your estate, and really plan out how the estate will be administered and what will happen. This is also a good opportunity to have a chat to your family members as well. Have a chat to your parents and really make sure that they are across this aspect of their own financial plan. If they haven't made appropriate plans, or if they haven't reviewed their estate plan, get them to seek appropriate advice to make sure things are administered in accordance with their wishes.

CONCLUSION:

Following Through on Your Financial Plan

Congratulations! You now have the financial skills and knowhow to steer yourself towards your dream life! While it may sound daunting, financial planning is all about being intentional with your money so you can live life the way you want to (rather than being on autopilot).

The key starting point is to get a solid understanding of your spending habits and set some tangible goals, so that you have a better idea of how much risk you want to take when it comes to investing your hard-earned cash. Thanks to the power of compounding, even small changes – like buying cheaper groceries or swapping takeaway coffee for homemade – can go a long way towards helping you grow your super or pay off your mortgage. Finally, having some emergency savings tucked away, together with taking care of income protection and estate planning, will make for a stress-free, financially secure future.

As you now know, there is a lot to consider when it comes to making financial decisions, so it is important to seek expert advice when you need some additional guidance. With the information laid out in this book, you'll be sure to get the most out of the experts you hire by asking the right questions. You will also know how to recognise advice that isn't right for you, as everything will now make a lot more sense.

Knowledge is potential; action is power.

TONY ROBBINS

Your biggest challenge now is not whether you earn enough money or have enough hours in the day to put your knowledge into action. Your biggest challenge is following through. So often, we start out with the best of intentions, yet we fail to act on those plans.

According to a survey by the Financial Planning Association of Australia (FPA), only twenty-three per cent of Australians believe they're 'living the dream'. So, what are they doing differently to everyone else? The FPA found that these people spent a lot more time visualising their future, were confident in their abilities to achieve what they wanted, and were focused and more likely to follow through with their plans. They were also more likely to seek the advice of a financial planner (twenty-four per cent) than those who describe themselves as not living the dream (nine per cent).

So, to help you get on the path to living your dream, I want to leave you with a few tips on what you can do to increase your chances of success.

Believe in Yourself

It can be really easy to tell ourselves why things can't be done, and to focus on all the things we should have done but haven't. But what we believe can often become a self-fulfilling prophecy. If you don't believe you have what it takes to achieve your goal, chances are you won't even try.

This is why the starting point to taking action is to believe you have the ability to achieve your goal. Focus on switching your thought process from being problem-focused to being solution-focused. Imagine if you were guaranteed to succeed in whatever you set out to do. What action would you take?

Starting out with this mindset, break down your goal into smaller, actionable steps. In other words, a to-do list. For example, rather than focusing on saving $10,000 by the end of the year, break this goal down into small steps. You can start by breaking it down into a weekly amount, so that it doesn't seem so daunting, and then break that down further to identify how you will find those savings. Here's how this might look:

Step 1: Figure out your weekly savings goal.
(Let's say you need to save $200 a week.)

Step 2: Review your spending for the last three months.

Step 3: Brainstorm ways you can cut back on spending by $200 a week.

Step 4: Commit to a new spending plan.

Step 5: Open a savings account.

Step 6: Ask payroll to transfer a portion of your pay into the savings account.

By starting to take small and easy steps, it will make the goal easier to attain and will motivate you to continue taking action.

Think About the Future

In my experience, a lot of people struggle to plan for the future. If I asked you what your plans are for this weekend or this month, chances are you would have a pretty good idea of what you are doing. The answer to that question becomes hazier the further off into the future we think. However, thinking about and planning for the future is a key component to achieving our dreams. A lack of vision for our future is a bit like getting in the car without knowing our destination – you may not like where you end up!

What I find helpful is to spend a little time each day dreaming about or visualising the future. Taking time out of the daily noise is a really important step to staying focused and motivated. Perhaps you might daydream about where you would like to live, or how you would like to spend your time each day, if it were completely up to you.

I remember when I first came to Australia, I regularly dreamed about what I wanted my life to look like some day – the investments I would have, the car I would drive, the work I would do. It really helped me get through the tough times and served as motivation to achieve my goals. Research has found that visualisation is a really powerful tool for helping you succeed. If you can picture yourself doing it, the odds are far greater that you actually will. If you can think it, you can do it!

Have a Failure Plan

Yes, you read that right. And no, I don't mean you should plan to fail. No matter how well mapped out your goals are, you can guarantee that it won't be a smooth journey getting there. Things won't always go your way. And sometimes your determination will be tested to the limits. And that's okay. Life isn't meant to be easy. However, if you don't mentally prepare yourself for the ups and downs, it can be really easy to give up on your dreams at the first sign of trouble.

This is why it is so important to put together a failure plan. In other words, when the going gets tough, how are you going to motivate yourself back into action? Is it by reading a book or speaking with a person that always inspires you and propels you forward? Is it by making a pact with yourself that you are allowed to feel sorry for yourself for a day or two, but will then commit to trying again? Write up a plan now so you can refer to it when you are feeling ready to give up.

Try to remember that when things don't go to plan, this is not a reflection on *you*. It does not mean that you are a failure. It does not mean that you are incapable. I am a big believer in things happening for a reason, and when things don't go our way it is usually because it wasn't the right fit for us and we needed to try a different approach or because there was a lesson we needed to take from the experience, to help us get to where we want to go.

When everything seems to be going against you,
remember that the plane takes off against the wind,
not with it.

Celebrate the Wins

Building wealth is a slow game and takes time, which means it can be really easy to get discouraged and lose sight of how far you have come. This is why – in order to truly believe in yourself and stay motivated – it's important to celebrate the wins, however small. Put together a plan now for how you will keep track of your progress and celebrate each milestone. Seeing that you are, in fact, making progress will motivate you to strive for even greater heights!

Surround Yourself with Like-Minded People

Changing our financial habits is no different to changing our eating or exercise habits. These goals are far more easily attained if you are surrounded by like-minded people who motivate you. At the start of the book, I mentioned the role our psychology plays with regard to habits, and our natural tendency to do what others are doing. This tendency can also be used to our advantage.

If you're trying to quit smoking, you're less likely to succeed if you surround yourself with other smokers, right? Or if you're trying to get fit and healthy, you may need to spend less time with friends who love cake and boozy nights out. The same rule applies to your financial habits.

If you have friends who are reckless with money, I'm not saying you should ditch them altogether. But try to find a network of like-minded people who can help you resist the temptation to spend money unnecessarily, and stay true to your goals. Our Women with Cents Facebook community is one example of such a network.

Remember, Your Future Depends on What You Do Today

This is just the beginning of your journey. I strongly encourage you to practise talking more about money – with your spouse, kids, parents and friends. The more you talk, think and learn about money, the more confidence you will have to do what it takes to achieve your dream lifestyle.

As the saying goes, you only live once. While money can't buy happiness, it certainly has the ability to impact your health, relationships and happiness. Living a busy schedule can make it easy to put your finances (and your life) on autopilot. I urge you not to let that happen.

Don't be a sitting duck in your own life and don't let outside forces determine what the future looks like for you. Take control of the wheel. There is more to life than just working to pay the bills, but we all have different definitions of what it means to be wealthy or financially free. Take some time to reflect on what financial freedom means to you, and don't be afraid to reach out for what you desire the most.

Also, don't shy away from seeking professional guidance when you need it. Trust your instincts, ask as many questions as you need, and don't be afraid to seek a second, third or fourth opinion if necessary.

Last but not least, keep in mind that the world of finance is constantly evolving, so it is important to stay up to date with current developments. If you would like to continue your journey of learning, be sure to sign up to our free newsletter at womenwithcents.com.au and join our online community.

And remember, your future depends on what you do today.

About the Author

Natasha Janssens is an award-winning financial planner, accountant and mortgage broker. After arriving in Australia as an eighteen-year-old refugee without her family, Natasha learned firsthand the complexities of navigating the Australian financial system and the challenges faced by Australian women.

Her passion for education and helping others led her to start Women with Cents – a finance business dedicated to empowering Australian women through education. Natasha is a regular contributor in the media, with her advice featured in numerous media outlets such as *Elle* magazine, *The Sydney Morning Herald*, ABC Radio, Mamamia and *Today Tonight*.

Through a combination of free resources, online courses, webinars, personal coaching and public events, Natasha has helped thousands of women across Australia facing various financial challenges, from a financially controlling partner or the risk of bankruptcy through to cutting back spending or pinpointing specific wealth-building strategies.

Natasha is on a mission to ensure that all Australian women have access to professional financial advice, regardless of their age, income or circumstances.

www.ingramcontent.com/pod-product-compliance
Lightning Source LLC
Chambersburg PA
CBHW071601210326
41597CB00019B/3340